Console Quest:
A History of Video Games Consoles

First & Second Generation

Charlie Robins

Contents

Introduction

Close your eyes and transport yourself to the year 1970, a time when household technology was limited to a mere handful of devices: a television set, a landline phone, and a wireless radio. Communication between people occurred over the fence, not through mobile phones. Mankind had just utilised the most complex technology to set foot on the moon.

Life back then was blissfully uncomplicated, free from the overwhelming influx of technical gizmos and gadgets that now engulf us. Fast forward to the present, and technology is omnipresent. We find ourselves surrounded by an array of sophisticated devices that have become an integral part of our daily lives.

Consider the smartphone in your pocket, a pocket-sized powerhouse of connectivity and productivity. Or the Wi-Fi-enabled TV that grants you access to a vast world of streaming entertainment, making movie nights more enjoyable. In the kitchen, a plethora of smart appliances has transformed cooking and baking into a breeze. I'm presently typing away on a laptop, a portable marvel that has revolutionized work and communication. And let's not forget the beloved video game console.

The video game console holds a special place in the evolution of household interactive technology. With controllers as input devices, you can witness a captivating output of data in the form of on-screen movement and sound. Without the invention of these consoles, our current world of personal interactive tech might have been vastly different.

At the forefront of this gaming revolution stands Ralph H. Baer, a visionary who explored the possibility of playing games on television sets while working for the defence contractor Sanders Associates. Collaborating with his colleagues Bill Harrison and Bill Rusch, Baer developed the first-ever prototype of a video game system called the "brown box" in 1967. After years of refining and searching for a potential buyer, the system was eventually licensed to electronics company Magnavox and rebranded as the Magnavox Odyssey. In 1972, it hit the market, making its mark as a "Pong console" that actually predated Atari's Pong System by several months.

Since the Odyssey's debut, home video gaming has undergone a remarkable transformation. Technological advancements have enabled manufacturers to enhance aspects like sound and colour variety. Simple gaming mechanics evolved into sophisticated platforms for immersive storytelling. The advent of online play connected players from all corners of the world with ease, solidifying the global dominance of video gaming.

In the 'Console Quest' book series, we embark on a journey through the fascinating history of home games consoles. 'Console Quest' comprises comprehensive lists of almost every home games console ever made, along with the history, statistics, and their accompanying video games. Delving into this book will enrich your understanding of gaming history, as well as providing gaming enthusiasts the satisfaction of ticking off consoles and video games they own. So, let's dive in and explore the captivating evolution of video game consoles that have shaped the way we play and experience games at home.

This book covers the first and second generations of games consoles, from the original Magnavox Odyssey to the iconic Atari 2600 and beyond.

FIRST GENERATION
1972-1980

Ralph Baer

Ralph H. Baer, often referred to as the "Father of Video Games," played a pivotal role in the development and creation of the Magnavox Odyssey, the world's first commercial home video game console. His innovative ideas and determination paved the way for the birth of the gaming industry as we know it today.

The story of the Magnavox Odyssey began in the mid-1960s when Ralph Baer was working as an engineer at Sanders Associates, a defense contractor company. In 1966, while waiting for a bus during his daily commute, Baer got a sudden burst of inspiration. He envisioned the potential of using television sets as a platform for interactive games, thus sparking the idea of creating a home video game console.

Baer, along with his colleagues Bill Harrison and Bill Rusch, started working on the prototype of the video game system, which they initially called the "brown box" due to its wooden casing. Over the next few years, Baer and his team devoted countless hours to refining and perfecting the concept.

The "brown box" prototype operated on a simple premise: players would use a set of controllers to interact with a series of light patterns displayed on a TV screen. The basic setup allowed for simple games like ping-pong and target shooting, where players controlled on-screen elements through knobs and switches.

By 1968, the "brown box" had evolved into a functional system capable of supporting multiple game variations. Baer saw the immense potential in this interactive entertainment device, and he began seeking opportunities to commercialize his invention.

In 1971, Baer demonstrated the "brown box" to various electronics companies, trying to find a partner interested in manufacturing and marketing the device. Eventually, his efforts paid off when he struck a deal with Magnavox, an established consumer electronics company.

The partnership led to the release of the Magnavox Odyssey in 1972, marking the official entry of video game consoles into the consumer market. The Odyssey, based on Baer's original concept, allowed players to enjoy a variety of simple games by overlaying transparent plastic sheets on the TV screen to create different playing fields.

Despite its initial success, the Odyssey faced certain limitations. Since the console did not have built-in circuitry to generate graphics, players had to use their imaginations to visualize the game scenarios based on the overlay patterns.

Nevertheless, the Magnavox Odyssey laid the foundation for future advancements in the gaming industry. Its significance lies in being the first commercially available video game console that brought interactive entertainment into people's homes.

Nolan Bushnell & Atari

Nolan Bushnell's fascination with technology and electronics began during his childhood. Born on February 5, 1943, in Clearfield, Utah, Bushnell showed an early interest in tinkering with machines and devices. This fascination only grew as he pursued an electrical engineering degree at the University of Utah.

While studying at the university, Bushnell was introduced to the world of computer programming and digital technology. He became enamored with the potential of computers and recognized their untapped potential for interactive entertainment. Bushnell's entrepreneurial instincts took root during this time, as he started to envision a future where people could play interactive games on computers.

After completing his education, Bushnell worked for various technology companies and gained experience in the burgeoning computer industry.

During his time working at a game manufacturer called Nutting Associates, Bushnell encountered a game called "Spacewar!"—an early digital computer game that captivated him. Inspired by "Spacewar!" and drawing from his passion for arcade games, he conceived the concept of creating a coin-operated arcade machine that would feature a simple yet addictive game.

With a vision in mind, Bushnell founded his own company, which he named Atari, inspired by the term "atari," used in the game "Go" to indicate a situation where a stone or group of stones is in danger of being captured.

In 1972, Bushnell and his friend Ted Dabney officially established Atari, Inc. Their first creation, the arcade game "Pong," quickly became a sensation. "Pong" was a simplified version of table tennis, where players controlled paddles and tried to hit a moving ball back and forth.

Arcades quickly became popular social gathering places, attracting teenagers and young adults seeking an exciting and social outlet. Players competed fiercely to achieve high scores and set records, fostering a competitive spirit that drove continued interest in arcade gaming.

The accessibility of gameplay and the curiosity surrounding this new form of entertainment drew crowds to arcades. With coin-operated machines, players could experience the thrill of gaming for a few minutes with each play, ensuring a steady flow of revenue for arcade operators.

While Bushnell did not have any direct involvement with the Magnavox Odyssey, the console's release and success played a crucial role in the early video game industry. The Odyssey's arrival in the market demonstrated the commercial viability of home video game consoles, inspiring Bushnell and Atari to capitalize on the emerging gaming trend.

Pong bore many similarities to one of the Odyssey's games, Table Tennis. While the concept of Pong was developed independently by Atari employee Allan Alcorn under Bushnell's direction, it is widely believed that the Odyssey's Table Tennis had some influence on the creation of Pong.

The success of "Pong" catapulted Atari into the gaming industry spotlight, and Bushnell's visionary leadership and innovative approach drove the company to develop more hit arcade games. Atari's games and arcade machines rapidly gained popularity, and the company became synonymous with video gaming during the 1970s and early 1980s.

In 1975, Atari entered the home console market with the release of the Atari Home Pong, an adaptation of the arcade game for home use. It was one of the first video game consoles designed for the mass market and laid the foundation for the home gaming revolution.

Technical Limitations

The consoles produced during the 1970s faced several significant technical limitations. These limitations were primarily due to the nascent state of video game technology and the available hardware during that era.

Consoles had very basic and limited processing power compared to modern gaming systems. The early microprocessors were not as advanced as today's CPUs, which restricted the complexity and sophistication of game graphics and mechanics.

Graphics capabilities were extremely basic and often limited to monochrome or simple black-and-white visuals. Players encountered simple shapes and characters rather than the colourful and detailed graphics seen in later generations.

The resolution of consoles was significantly lower than what we see in modern gaming. Game screens were composed of a limited number of pixels, resulting in blocky and pixelated images.

Early game consoles had fixed, hardwired game logic, meaning that the games they could play were limited to what was built into the console's hardware. There was no ability to change or update game content like modern downloadable content (DLC).

Memory capacity was very constrained. This limited the amount of data that could be stored, including graphics, sound, and game states, leading to simple and short games.

Sound in early consoles was minimal, often limited to simple beeps and tones. There was no capacity for background music or complex audio effects.

Unlike modern consoles that can run various games through interchangeable cartridges or digital downloads, first-generation consoles had dedicated hardware for specific games. To play a different game, users needed a separate console or machine.

Input devices, such as paddles or joysticks, used to control games were basic and lacked complexity. These simple input methods restricted the range of gameplay actions.

Pong Clones

Pongs immense popularity and success in arcades led to a wave of imitation and variation games consoles, commonly known as Pong clones.

Numerous companies sought to capitalize on the arcade gaming craze ignited by Pong. As a result, they created their own versions of the game, often with slight modifications or enhancements to differentiate their product while still maintaining the core gameplay mechanics.

Pong clones varied in terms of visual presentation, sound effects, and additional features. Some clones added new game modes or increased the game's difficulty, while others introduced different themes or graphics to appeal to specific audiences. Although Pong clones shared similarities with the original game, they were not direct copies or pirated versions, as many companies developed their clones independently.

Cloning Pong became common due to several factors. Pong's straightforward gameplay and simple mechanics made it relatively easy for other developers to replicate. The video game industry was still in its early stages, and intellectual property laws were less stringent at the time, allowing for greater flexibility in game creation.

As the popularity of arcade gaming continued to grow, the abundance of Pong clones flooded the market. This led to intense competition, resulting in a wide array of similar games vying for players' attention. Some clones managed to find success and developed their own dedicated following, while others faded into obscurity.

Lack of Handhelds

During the first generation, home video game consoles were still in their infancy, with manufacturers focused on perfecting and commercializing stationary gaming systems for televisions. The primary goal was to bring gaming experiences to the living room, where players could enjoy them on larger screens and with more advanced hardware capabilities.

Technological constraints played a significant role in the absence of handheld consoles. The computing power required to deliver satisfactory gaming experiences was not yet miniaturized enough to fit into portable devices. Components like processors, memory, and display technologies were bulkier and less power-efficient, making it challenging to create compact, battery-powered handheld gaming devices with satisfactory performance.

The market demand and consumer expectations for portable gaming were not as pronounced during the first generation. Home consoles were gaining popularity, and the focus was primarily on bringing gaming experiences to the comfort of the living room. The concept of portable gaming was relatively nascent, and the demand for handheld consoles had not yet reached a critical mass.

The production and distribution infrastructure required to support handheld consoles were not as advanced during the first generation. Manufacturing processes, supply chains, and marketing strategies were primarily tailored to stationary home consoles, which were already gaining traction and market acceptance.

The first generation of games consoles laid the foundation for the subsequent generations, where advancements in technology, shifting consumer preferences, and evolving market dynamics would propel the rise of handheld gaming. These factors, along with the maturation of portable technology and the emergence of more powerful and compact components, would eventually pave the way for the birth of handheld consoles in subsequent generations.

The Ending of the First generation

Eventually the market became saturated with various Pong clones and other simple games. With many companies producing similar games, the novelty of arcade gaming started to wane, and consumers sought something new and innovative.

As technology progressed, the limitations of the first-generation consoles became increasingly apparent. Players demanded more sophisticated graphics, sound capabilities, and gameplay mechanics that the early consoles couldn't provide. As gamers sought more complex and diverse gaming experiences, the first-generation consoles no longer met consumer demands. The industry needed to adapt to cater to the evolving preferences of players.

Arcades continued to evolve with the advent of more powerful hardware and innovative games. The focus shifted from Pong-style games to titles with more engaging visuals and gameplay, further distancing arcades from the first-generation simplicity.

The introduction of the second generation of video game consoles signalled the end of the first generation. Consoles like the Fairchild Channel F (released in 1976) and the more influential Atari 2600 (originally known as the Atari VCS, released in 1977) brought significant advancements in gaming technology and software capabilities. The second generation of consoles shifted the focus from dedicated Pong-style machines to versatile home gaming systems. The Atari 2600 allowed for interchangeable game cartridges, giving players a wide selection of games without needing separate consoles for each title.

This chapter contains information on notable consoles released during this time, as well as a list of all consoles released during the first generation.

Home Consoles

☐Magnavox Odyssey

RELEASE DATE	USA: September 1972
	EU: 1973
DISCONTINUED	1975
ORIGINAL PRICE	$100
UNITS SOLD	350,000

Developed by Ralph Baer and released by Magnavox in 1972, the Odyssey paved the way for the entire video game industry. The Odyssey was the first commercially available home video game console. It was initially released as the "Brown Box" during its development stage and was later rebranded as the Odyssey upon its official release.

Unlike modern video game consoles that use microprocessors and digital graphics, the Odyssey used analog circuitry to produce simple, black-and-white graphics on a standard television.

The Odyssey came with a set of plastic overlays and accessories to play various games, but it had a very limited library of games. The games included simple variations of Pong, tennis, and shooting games. The console itself was a box with knobs and switches on the front. Players used these controls to manipulate the on-screen elements. The system required players to connect it to a television and adjust settings manually for each game.

The system was primarily designed for two players to interact with each other, as it lacked AI opponents. The system encouraged players to be creative and use their imagination in their gameplay.

The Odyssey had a slow start in the market. Despite being a groundbreaking product, it faced challenges in marketing, with consumers often being unsure of what exactly the system could do. It was also relatively expensive. The console eventually went on to sell around 350,000 units.

Magnavox Odyssey Series

The Odyssey series includes eight specialized home video game consoles and one television featuring a built-in game console. These gaming platforms were all introduced in the United States by Magnavox following its acquisition by Philips in 1974. Odyssey consoles were released under the Philips brand in Europe. Unlike the original Odyssey, which used a printed circuit board, the Series of systems used inbuild chips to function. Between 1972 and 1981, Magnavox sold over 1.7 million gaming systems under the Odyssey brand.

☐Magnavox Odyssey 100

RELEASE DATE	USA: October 1975
ORIGINAL PRICE	$99.95
GAMES INCLUDED	Hockey Tennis
NUMBER OF PLAYERS	2
POWER SUPPLY	6x C batteries 9V AC Adaptor

☐ Magnavox/ Philips Odyssey 200

RELEASE DATE	USA: November 1975 EU: 1976
ORIGINAL PRICE	$129.95
GAMES INCLUDED	Hockey Smash Tennis
NUMBER OF PLAYERS	2
POWER SUPPLY	6x C batteries 9V AC Adaptor

◻Magnavox
Odyssey 300

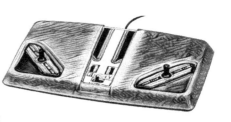

RELEASE DATE	USA: October 1976
ORIGINAL PRICE	$69.00
GAMES INCLUDED	Hockey Smash Tennis
NUMBER OF PLAYERS	2
POWER SUPPLY	6x C batteries 9V AC Adaptor

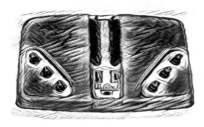

◻ Magnavox
Odyssey 400

RELEASE DATE	USA: 1976
ORIGINAL PRICE	$100.00
GAMES INCLUDED	Hockey Smash Tennis
NUMBER OF PLAYERS	2
POWER SUPPLY	6x C batteries 9V AC Adaptor

◻Magnavox
Odyssey 500

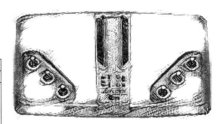

RELEASE DATE	USA: 1976
ORIGINAL PRICE	$130.00
GAMES INCLUDED	Hockey Smash Soccer Tennis
NUMBER OF PLAYERS	2
POWER SUPPLY	6x C batteries 9V AC Adaptor

☐Magnavox Odyssey 4305 (Inbuilt TV)

RELEASE DATE	USA: October 1976
ORIGINAL PRICE	$499.00
GAMES INCLUDED	Hockey Smash Tennis
NUMBER OF PLAYERS	2
POWER SUPPLY	Mains power

☐ Magnavox/ Philips Odyssey 2000

RELEASE DATE	USA: 1977
	EU: 1977
ORIGINAL PRICE	N/A
GAMES INCLUDED	Hockey Practice Smash Tennis
NUMBER OF PLAYERS	1/2
POWER SUPPLY	6x C batteries 9V AC Adaptor

☐Magnavox Odyssey 3000

RELEASE DATE	USA: 1977
ORIGINAL PRICE	N/A
GAMES INCLUDED	Hockey Practice Smash Tennis
NUMBER OF PLAYERS	1/2
POWER SUPPLY	6x C batteries 9V AC Adaptor

☐Magnavox
Odyssey 4000

RELEASE DATE	USA: 1977
GAMES INCLUDED	Basketball
	Hockey
	Gridball
	Practice
	Smash
	Soccer
	Tennis
NUMBER OF PLAYERS	1/2
POWER SUPPLY	9V AC Adaptor

☐ Philips
Odyssey 2001

RELEASE DATE	EU: 1977
GAMES INCLUDED	Hockey
	Squash
	Tennis
NUMBER OF PLAYERS	1/2
POWER SUPPLY	6x C batteries
	9V AC Adaptor

☐Philips
Odyssey 2100

RELEASE DATE	EU: 1978
GAMES INCLUDED	Flipper
	Football
	Handball
	Ice Hockey
	Tennis
	Wipeout
NUMBER OF PLAYERS	1/2
POWER SUPPLY	6x C batteries
	9V AC Adaptor

☐Epoch Co. TV Tennis Electrotennis

RELEASE DATE	JP: September 1975
DISCONTINUED	N/A
ORIGINAL PRICE	¥19,000
GAMES INCLUDED	Tennis
UNITS SOLD	N/A

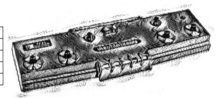

The TV Tennis Electrotennis, was introduced by Epoch Co. in cooperation with Magnavox on September 12, 1975, exclusively in Japan, with a price tag of 19,000 Japanese yen. It marked the very first video game console release in Japan, predating North America's Home Pong by several months.

An exceptional feature of the TV Tennis Electrotennis was its wireless connection to a television, functioning via a UHF antenna. Estimates of its total sales vary from approximately 10,000 to 20,000 units, or even as high as 3 million units over its lifetime.

Atari Home Pong Series

As early as 1974, Atari embarked on the design of a home version of their PONG arcade machine. This system was a collaborative effort among engineers Harold Lee, Alan Alcorn, and Bob Brown.

Atari faced rejection from toy and electronics manufacturers, as other gaming systems were not experiencing significant sales. It was during this time that one of Atari's directors reached out to Tom Quinn, an individual working at Sears/Roebuck. After several meetings with Atari founder Nolan Bushnell, Sears placed an order for 150,000 PONG systems to be ready for the Christmas season. These systems, assembled by Atari, were sold under the Sears Tele-Games label. Atari went on to release their own branded version of the console.

Home Pong offered a simplified version of table tennis or ping-pong. Players controlled paddles on the screen to hit a ball back and forth. The goal was to score points by making the ball pass your opponent's paddle. The primary mode of play in Home Pong was for two players. Each player had a controller with a knob to move their paddle up and down.

Home Pong displayed very basic and monochromatic graphics on the television screen. It typically had simple backgrounds and a straightforward representation of the ball and paddles. The console had basic sound effects, including simple beeps and blips that accompanied the on-screen action.

Home Pong was a massive success upon its release. It was an affordable and accessible way for people to enjoy video games at home. It paved the way for the video game industry's growth in the late 1970s.

Different models of home Pong consoles were released with slight variations in gameplay. Some offered features like adjustable ball speed or the ability to play against the computer in single-player mode. The partnership between Atari and Sears produced other dedicated consoles such as Hockey, Speedway, Pinball Breakaway, Stunt Cycle, and Motocross.

☐Atari Pong

RELEASE DATE	1976
ORIGINAL PRICE	$55.00
GAMES INCLUDED	Pong
NUMBER OF PLAYERS	2
POWER SUPPLY	4x D batteries AC Adaptor

☐Atari Pong Doubles

RELEASE DATE	Unreleased
ORIGINAL PRICE	N/A
GAMES INCLUDED	Pong
NUMBER OF PLAYERS	4
POWER SUPPLY	4x D batteries AC Adaptor

☐Atari Super Pong

RELEASE DATE	1976
ORIGINAL PRICE	$79.95
GAMES INCLUDED	Catch Pong Solitaire Super Pong
NUMBER OF PLAYERS	2
POWER SUPPLY	4x D batteries 9V AC Adaptor

☐Atari Super Pong Ten

RELEASE DATE	1976
ORIGINAL PRICE	N/A
GAMES INCLUDED	Basketball
	Catch
	Handball
	Pong
	Super Pong
NUMBER OF PLAYERS	4
POWER SUPPLY	4x D batteries
	AC Adaptor

☐Atari Super Pong Pro-Am

RELEASE DATE	1977
ORIGINAL PRICE	N/A
GAMES INCLUDED	Pong
NUMBER OF PLAYERS	2
POWER SUPPLY	4x D batteries
	AC Adaptor

☐Atari Super Pong Pro-Am Ten

RELEASE DATE	1977
ORIGINAL PRICE	N/A
GAMES INCLUDED	Basketball
	Catch
	Handball
	Pong
	Super Pong
NUMBER OF PLAYERS	4
POWER SUPPLY	4x D batteries
	AC Adaptor

☐Atari Ultra Pong/Ultra Pong Doubles

RELEASE DATE	1977
ORIGINAL PRICE	N/A
GAMES INCLUDED	pong
	super pong
	hyper pong
	ultra pong
	hockey
	super hockey
	hyper hockey
	ultra hockey
	barrier pong
	super barrier pong
	hyper barrier pong
	ultra barrier pong
	barrier hockey
	super barrier hockey
	hyper barrier hockey
	ultra barrier hockey
NUMBER OF PLAYERS	2/4
POWER SUPPLY	4x C batteries
	5.5v AC Adaptor

☐Sears Tele-Games Pong

RELEASE DATE	1975
ORIGINAL PRICE	N/A
GAMES INCLUDED	Pong
NUMBER OF PLAYERS	2
POWER SUPPLY	4x D batteries
	AC Adaptor

Sears Tele-Games Pong IV

RELEASE DATE	1975
ORIGINAL PRICE	N/A
GAMES INCLUDED	Pong
NUMBER OF PLAYERS	4
POWER SUPPLY	4x D batteries AC Adaptor

Sears Tele-Games Super Pong IV

RELEASE DATE	1977
ORIGINAL PRICE	N/A
GAMES INCLUDED	Basketball Catch Handball Pong Super Pong
NUMBER OF PLAYERS	2/4
POWER SUPPLY	4x D batteries AC Adaptor

☐Sears Tele-Games Pong Sports II

RELEASE DATE	1977
GAMES INCLUDED	pong
	super pong
	hyper pong
	ultra pong
	hockey
	super hockey
	hyper hockey
	ultra hockey
	barrier pong
	super barrier pong
	hyper barrier pong
	ultra barrier pong
	barrier hockey
	super barrier hockey
	hyper barrier hockey
	ultra barrier hockey
NO. OF PLAYERS	2
POWER SUPPLY	4x D batteries
	AC Adaptor

☐Sears Tele-Games Pong Sports IV

RELEASE DATE	1977
GAMES INCLUDED	pong
	super pong
	hyper pong
	ultra pong
	hockey
	super hockey
	hyper hockey
	ultra hockey
	barrier pong
	super barrier pong
	hyper barrier pong
	ultra barrier pong
	barrier hockey
	super barrier hockey
	hyper barrier hockey
	ultra barrier hockey
NO. OF PLAYERS	4
POWER SUPPLY	4x D batteries
	AC Adaptor

☐Sears Tele-Games Hockey-Pong

RELEASE DATE	1977
ORIGINAL PRICE	N/A
GAMES INCLUDED	Hockey Pong
NUMBER OF PLAYERS	2
POWER SUPPLY	4x D batteries AC Adaptor

Coleco Telstar Series

Coleco (Connecticut Leather Company) was a company known for manufacturing leather products, but they entered the video game console market with the Telstar series as part of the early wave of home video gaming. The Telstar consoles were relatively simple and offered a range of Pong-style games and other variations. The systems typically offered options like tennis, hockey, and squash, which were essentially different versions of the same ball-and-paddle gameplay.

The first Telstar model was introduced in 1976 and marked Coleco's entry into the video game industry. Several variations of the Telstar were released in the years that followed, such as the Telstar Classic, Telstar Deluxe, and Telstar Ranger. Each model offered slightly different games and features.

The Telstar consoles were very basic in terms of graphics and gameplay. They used analog circuitry to generate the graphics, and the games were displayed in black and white or with very simple colour overlays. The consoles usually came with detachable controllers featuring rotary dials or paddles for players to control the on-screen action. Some Telstar models had pistol-style light guns for shooting games.

The Telstar series was reasonably successful for Coleco during the late 1970s, particularly due to its affordability and simplicity, making it accessible to a wide audience. However The popularity of the Telstar consoles waned as more advanced and versatile video game systems, like the Atari 2600, entered the market. These newer systems offered a wider range of interchangeable games and more advanced graphics. By the early 1980s, the Coleco Telstar series had largely faded from the video game market as the industry continued to evolve.

Approximately 1 million Telstar units were sold during the system's lifespan.

Coleco Telstar

RELEASE DATE	1976
ORIGINAL PRICE	N/A
GAMES INCLUDED	Handball
	Hockey
	Tennis
NUMBER OF PLAYERS	2
POWER SUPPLY	6x C batteries
	AC Adaptor

Coleco Telstar Classic

RELEASE DATE	1976
ORIGINAL PRICE	N/A
GAMES INCLUDED	Handball
	Hockey
	Tennis
NUMBER OF PLAYERS	2
POWER SUPPLY	6x C batteries
	AC Adaptor

Coleco Telstar Deluxe, AKA Video World of Sports

RELEASE DATE	CA: 1977
ORIGINAL PRICE	N/A
GAMES INCLUDED	Handballs
	Hockey
	Tennis ball
NUMBER OF PLAYERS	2
POWER SUPPLY	6x C batteries
	AC Adaptor

☐Coleco Telstar Ranger

RELEASE DATE	1977
ORIGINAL PRICE	N/A
GAMES INCLUDED	Handball Hockey Jai alai Skeet Target Tennis
NUMBER OF PLAYERS	2
POWER SUPPLY	6x C batteries AC Adaptor

☐Coleco Telstar Alpha

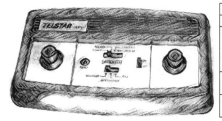

RELEASE DATE	1977
ORIGINAL PRICE	N/A
GAMES INCLUDED	Handball Hockey Squash Tennis
NUMBER OF PLAYERS	2
POWER SUPPLY	6x C batteries AC Adaptor

☐Coleco Telstar Colormatic

RELEASE DATE	1977
ORIGINAL PRICE	N/A
GAMES INCLUDED	Handball Hockey Jai alai Tennis
NUMBER OF PLAYERS	2
POWER SUPPLY	6x C batteries

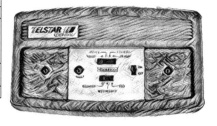

☐Coleco Telstar Regent

RELEASE DATE	1977
ORIGINAL PRICE	N/A
GAMES INCLUDED	Handball
	Hockey
	Jai alai
	Tennis
NUMBER OF PLAYERS	2
POWER SUPPLY	6x C batteries

☐Coleco Telstar Combat!

RELEASE DATE	1977
ORIGINAL PRICE	N/A
GAMES INCLUDED	Camouflage Combat
	Combat
	Night Battle
	Robot Battle
NUMBER OF PLAYERS	2
POWER SUPPLY	6x C batteries
	AC Adaptor

☐Coleco Telstar Galaxy

RELEASE DATE	1977
ORIGINAL PRICE	N/A
GAMES INCLUDED	Basketball
	Foosball
	Handball
	Hockey
	Soccer
	Tennis
NUMBER OF PLAYERS	1/2
POWER SUPPLY	AC Adaptor

□Coleco Telstar Gemini

RELEASE DATE	1977
ORIGINAL PRICE	N/A
GAMES INCLUDED	4x Pinball games 2x Light Gun games
NUMBER OF PLAYERS	2
POWER SUPPLY	AC Adaptor

□Coleco Telstar Arcade

RELEASE DATE	1977
ORIGINAL PRICE	N/A
NUMBER OF PLAYERS	1/2
POWER SUPPLY	AC Adaptor

Games List

- Twenty-five game driving maze
- Pack-in game

- Five-game pinball and shooting
- Fifteen-game action

- Eight-game ball and target
- Battle game

□Coleco Telstar Sportsman

RELEASE DATE	1978
ORIGINAL PRICE	N/A
GAMES INCLUDED	6x Light gun games
NUMBER OF PLAYERS	1/2
POWER SUPPLY	AC Adaptor

☐Coleco Telstar Colortron

RELEASE DATE	1978
ORIGINAL PRICE	N/A
GAMES INCLUDED	Handball
	Hockey
	Jai alai
	Tennis
NUMBER OF PLAYERS	2
POWER SUPPLY	2x 9V batteries
	AC Adaptor

☐Coleco Telstar Marksman

RELEASE DATE	1978
ORIGINAL PRICE	N/A
GAMES INCLUDED	Handball
	Hockey
	Jai alai
	Skeet
	Target
	Tennis
NUMBER OF PLAYERS	2
POWER SUPPLY	2x 9V batteries
	AC Adaptor

Nintendo Color TV-Game Series

The Nintendo Color TV-Game series was a line of dedicated home video game consoles produced by Nintendo, It was one of the company's earliest forays into the video game industry before they became widely known for systems like the Nintendo Entertainment System (NES). The Color TV-Game series was primarily available in Japan.

Hiroshi Yamauchi, the president of Nintendo at the time, was looking for ways to diversify the company's product offerings. Nintendo, originally a playing card company, had already ventured into various businesses, including toys and instant rice, before entering the video game market.

Nintendo collaborated with Mitsubishi Electric, a major Japanese conglomerate, to develop these early video game consoles. Mitsubishi was a leader in electronic technology, and their expertise was crucial in creating the Color TV-Game series.

The idea behind the Color TV-Game series was to create simple, affordable, and accessible video game consoles that would appeal to a broad audience. At the time, video games were mostly found in arcades, and Nintendo aimed to bring the arcade experience to the living room.

The Color TV-Game series was first introduced in 1977, and it consisted of several models that each played a specific game or set of games. Some of the more popular models in the series included the Color TV-Game 6, Color TV-Game 15, and Color TV-Game Racing 112. The number in the model name indicated the number of games included.

The Color TV-Game series' games were typically very basic in terms of graphics and gameplay. The consoles used paddle controllers that players could use to control the on-screen action. These controllers were often built into the console itself.

Approximately 3 million units were sold during the system's lifespan. While the Color TV-Game series was relatively simple and short-lived (the range was discontinued in 1983), it marked Nintendo's early venture into the video game market. Today, the Color TV-Game consoles are considered collector's items and have historical significance in the evolution of video gaming.

☐Nintendo Color TV-Game 6

RELEASE DATE	JP: June 1977
ORIGINAL PRICE	¥9,800
GAMES INCLUDED	6x Light Tennis variations
NUMBER OF PLAYERS	2
POWER SUPPLY	Batteries AC Adaptor

☐Nintendo Color TV-Game 15

RELEASE DATE	JP: June 1977
ORIGINAL PRICE	¥15,000
GAMES INCLUDED	15x Light Tennis variations
NUMBER OF PLAYERS	2
POWER SUPPLY	Batteries AC Adaptor

☐Nintendo Color TV-Game Racing 112

RELEASE DATE	JP: June 1978
ORIGINAL PRICE	¥12,000
GAMES INCLUDED	112x top down racing variations
NUMBER OF PLAYERS	1
POWER SUPPLY	Batteries AC Adaptor

☐Nintendo Color TV-Game
Block Kuzushi

RELEASE DATE	JP: April 1979
ORIGINAL PRICE	¥13,500
GAMES INCLUDED	6x Breakout variations
NUMBER OF PLAYERS	1
POWER SUPPLY	AC Adaptor

☐Nintendo Computer TV-Game

RELEASE DATE	JP: 1980
ORIGINAL PRICE	N/A
GAMES INCLUDED	Computer Othello
NUMBER OF PLAYERS	2
POWER SUPPLY	AC Adaptor

First Generation Full Console List

1972

- Magnavox
  - Odyssey

1973

- ITT Schaub-Lorenz
  - Odyssee
- Inter Electrónica
  - Overkal

1974

- Henry's
  - VideoSport MK2
- Interton
  - Video 2000
- Videomaster
  - Home TV Game VM 577
- Zanussi
  - Ping-O-Tronic

1975

- Alcatel
  - Visiomatic 101
- Commodore
  - TV Game 2000K
- Epoch Co.
  - TV Tennis Electrotennis
- Executive Games
  - Television Tennis (35)
- First Dimension
  - Video System FD-3000W
- Koninklijke Philips NV
  - Tele-Spiel ES-2201
- Magnavox
  - Odyssey 100
  - Odyssey 200
- Sears Tele-Games
  - Pong (model 25796)
- Sears Tele-Games
  - Pong IV (99717)
- Société occitane d'électronique
  - Occitel

- Universal Research Laboratories
  - Video Action VA-II
- Videomaster
  - Home TV Game MK2 (VM 577)
  - Home TV Game MK3 (VM3)
  - Olympic (VM3 MK2)
  - Rally (VM4 MK1)

1976

- Allied's
  - Name Of The Game (A-100)
  - Name of the Game II (A-300)
- APF Electronics
  - TV Fun 401
- Atari
  - Pong (model C-100)
- Binatone
  - TV-Tron (01-4982)
- BMC
  - Video Game TVG-5000
- Canadian Tire
  - Video Sports 84-6072
- Coleco
  - Telstar
  - Telstar Classic
- E&P
  - Electronic TV Game EP 460
  - Electronic TV Game EP500
- EA
  - TV-Ping-Pong (DN76)
- Executive Games
  - Face Off
- First Dimension
  - Video Sports 76
  - Video Sports 76c
- FKF
  - TV Games Model 100 TV Spiel
- Gemini
  - 7640

- General Home Products
  - Magnavox Wonder Wizard (7702)
  - Wonder Wizard, Bulls Eye (7704)
  - Wonder Wizard, Scoreboard (7706)
  - Wonder Wizard, Sharp Shooter (7705)
- Glorytone
  - Video Olympiad
- Granada Electronics
  - Video Olympiad
  - Video Sports
- GTE
  - Tele Pong
  - Tele Pong IV
- Gulliver
- Triple Challenge 7701
- Heathkit
  - GD-1380
  - GD-1999
- IEA
  - Tele-Tainment
  - Tele-Tainment II
- Interton
  - Video 3000
- Koninklijke Philips NV
  - Odyssey 200
- Lloyd's
  - TV-Sports 801 (mod.E801)
- Magnavox
  - Odyssey 300
  - Odyssey 400
  - Odyssey 4305
  - Odyssey 500
- Mecca
  - EP-460
  - EP-500
- Mestron
  - Fernseh Spiel TVG 2006
  - Mec TV Games TVG 1000
- Monteverdi
  - TV Sport 825
- National Semiconductor
  - Adversary 370

- Orelec
  - PP-2000
- Packet Instrument
  - TV Sport
- Playtech
  - Telesport TV Games
- Prinztronic
  - Tournament TV Game Electronic (VM8)
- RadioShack
  - TV Scoreboard 60-3051
  - TV Scoreboard 60-3052
- Ricochet Electronics
  - Electronic Color TV Game Center (MT-1A)
  - Formula 500 (MT-5A)
- Roberts
  - Paddle IV
  - Paddle VI
- Sears
  - Tele-Games Hockey-Pong (99721)
  - Tele-Games Super Pong IV (99737)
- Société occitane d'électronique
  - OC4 Société Occitane d'Electronique
- Superlectron
- TV Challenger Series 2000
- Tele-Match
  - Tele-Match 4 (model 4400)
  - Tele-Match Concert Hall IV (model 8800)
- Teletenis
  - Multijuegos
- Teyboll
  - Automatico

- Unisonic Products
  - Corporation Sportsman T101
  - Corporation Tournament 100
  - Corporation Tournament 102
  - Corporation Tournament 150
  - Corporation Tournament 200
- Universal Research Laboratories
  - Video Action IV Indy 500 (S-100)
  - Video Action TV Game 1000
  - Video Action VA-III
- Universum
  - Multi-Spiel Color
  - TV-Multi-Spiel
- Venture Electronics
  - Video Sports VS-1
- Videomaster
  - Superscore (VM-8)
- Videoton
  - Elektronikus TV játék
- Windsor
  - TV Game EP500
- Y.S.A.
  - Sport King Model-101

1977

- A.G.S. Electronics Ltd.
  - TVG 101-4
- Academy
  - D-5996 Programmable TV Game Console
  - Most Exciting Home Video Game (D-5614)
  - TVG-406-6
  - Video Game (D-5654)
  - Video Game (D-5715)
- Acetronic
  - Sports-Action TV Game 922

- Ajax
  - Color Video Game BM-1000
  - TV Game (TVG-406-6)
  - TV Game AU-807
  - TV Game T-800
- Akur
  - TVG-SD-01-8 Color
- Alex Video Spiel
  - TG-621
- Algemene Bank Nederland
  - TV Spel AU-807
  - TV Spel T-338
- Alltronic
  - Electronic TV Game Centre Model 15
  - HK 1350
- Ameltone
  - Most Exciting Home Video Game D-5614
  - Stadium 4002
  - Stadium BW-11
  - Stadium C-4003
  - Stadium Colour C-22
  - TVG-SD-01
  - TV Fun 401A
  - TV Fun 405a
  - TV Fun 406
  - TV Fun 442
  - TV Fun Match 405
  - TV Fun Sportsarama 402 - 402C
- Asaflex
  - Asaflex 6
  - Video Sports
  - Video Sports 2000
- Atari
  - Video Pinball C-380 (white)
  - Video Pinball C-380 (woodgrain)
- Atomic
  - TV-Player I
  - TV-Player II

- Audiosonic
  - Home TV Set PP-600
  - Most Exciting Home Video Game PP-420
  - PP-800
  - PP-900
- Bandai
  - TV JACK 1000
  - TV JACK 1200
  - TV JACK 1500
  - TV JACK 2500
  - TV JACK 3000
- Bang Bang Electronic
  - TV Master Mark II
- Bemor
  - Gamatic 7600
- Bianchi
  - SA Telesport
- Binatone
  - TV Gaming Unit (01-4990)
  - TV Master 4 plus 2 (01-4869)
  - TV Master MK 10 (01-4834)
  - TV Master MK 6 (01-4907)
  - TV Master MK 8 (01-4823)
  - TV Master Mk IV (01-4974)
- Bingo
  - TVG-203
  - TVG-204
  - TVG-205
  - Video Game HI-1012
- Blaupunkt
  - Telejuego
  - TV Action Color 100
  - TV Action Color 200
- BMC
  - Video Action TVG-9000 Grand Prix 77
- Bonny
  - TV Game AU-807
- Boots
  - Audio TG100
- Bowmar
  - Bang 1000
- Brandt Electronique
  - Jeu Video JT 321

- C&G Electronic
  - Breamcolor
  - Breamcross
  - Teleplay (Bream Player Special)
- C.I.C.
  - TVG 101-4
  - TVG 201-4
  - TVG-406-6
- C.V.T. Industries Ltd.
  - Videosport
- Cabel Electronic
  - Lem 2000
- Calfax
  - Bag-A-Tel Ep-800
- Carinco
  - SD-081
- Coleco
  - Combat!
  - Telstar Alpha
  - Telstar Arcade
  - Telstar Colormatic
  - Telstar Deluxe
  - Telstar Galaxy
  - Telstar Ranger
  - Telstar Regent
- Comersa
  - Videosport 4000
  - Videosport 4000 Color
  - Videosport Junior
- Commodore
  - TV Game 3000H
- Concept 2000
  - Nose T' Nose, 4-way videogame
  - Spectrum 6 (1025)
  - TV4+ Four-Way Video Game
- Concord
  - Telejeu 6000
  - TVG-205 colour
  - Video Game TVG-203
- Conic
  - 304
  - 4A-8 (9015)
  - 6 game TV game - TVG 4010-6
  - Colour Video Game
  - DX-702
  - Heroic Tank
  - MPC-862C - Programmable TV Game
  - TV Sports TG-621
  - TV Sports TG-721

- TVG 101-4
  - TVG 102-4
  - TVG 201-4
  - TVG 202-4
  - TVG 204-4
  - TVG 209
  - TVG 406-6
  - TVG-SD-01
- Consolidate Enterprises
  - Convoy 7600
- Continental Edison
  - Jeux Video JV-2701
  - Jeux Video JV-2703
  - Jeux Video JV-2705
- Jeux Video JV-2707
- Controlmetrics
  - Video Esport
- Cosinus
  - Color TV game 4000c
- Creatronic
  - Bi.Bip 4
  - Bi.Bip 6
  - Bi.Bip 8
- Daewoo
  - TV-Sports 77
- Davitronix
  - 7N tv game
  - Video Sport
- Dayya Corp.
  - Marumé 2000 (VM-90C)
- Dazzla
  - TV-Games 007
- Decca
  - Programmable Video Game System
  - Sport TV Game Colour TG-0062
  - Sport TV Game monochrome
- Deportel
  - Deportel
- Derby Master
  - Multi Color 777 (777-JS)
- Diasonic
  - TV Game HVG-220
  - TV Game Y-1170
- Dick Smith
  - Y-1170 TV Game

- Digitek
  - TV Game 2001
- DKS
  - Color TV sports TVG-406-6
- DS-2
  - DS-2
- E&P Electronic LTD.
  - Electronic TV Sport Games EP800
- EACA
  - Hide-Away TV Game
- Echo Electronics Corporation
  - TV-Games LU-009
- Elbex
  - Programmable 2003
- Electrophonic
  - Pro-Sports TVG-1001
- Elftone
  - D-5614
  - El-tvg-01
  - El-tvg-02c
- Elpro
  - POC-POC 2007
- Enterprex
  - Apollo 2001 Color Home Video Game
  - Apollo 2004 Color Home Video Game
- Epoch Co.
  - TV Game System 10
- Evadin TVG 102-4
- Exclusiv
  - Color TVG-409 - 4/8
- FS-Spiel
  - TVG-204 - 4/8
  - TVG-209 – 4
- Eximec
  - TV-Spiel Color 1
  - TV-Spiel Color 2
- Fuji Electric
  - Sportstron TV-Game (Coca-Cola edition)

- Furtec
  - Furtec 4 (TVG-30)
  - Furtec 5
  - Furtec 6 (TVG-10)
- General Home Products
  - WonderWizard (7709)
- Glendearg
  - Electrosport Colour
- Gorenje
  - Geti-3220
- Gracia
  - Color Video Game TVG-432
  - TV Game R-1800
- Granada Electronics
  - TV Game EP500
  - TV Game EP800
- Grandstand
  - Adman Sportsvision TV Game Model 1000
  - Adman TVG-2600 MK II
  - Colour Video Sports Centre 4600 DeLuxe
  - Match of the Day 2000
  - TV game color Adman 3000
- Groupe SEB
  - Telescore 750
  - Telescore 751
  - Telescore 752
- Grundig
  - Tank Battle
- Hanimex
  - 7771-G
  - 7771-P
  - 888
  - Colour TV Game 8881
  - Electronic TV Game 777
  - Jeu-Tele Electronique Modèle 7771
  - TV Scoreboard 888G
  - TVG-500
  - TVG-801
- Harvard
  - Tank Battle TV Game H-7
- Harvey
  - TVG-406-6

- Heru Ellipses
  - TV Sport (T-338)
  - TVG-621
- HGS Electronic
  - Telematch TV Sports Color video game
- Hitachi
  - VG-104
- Hit-Go
  - TVG-203
- Hobbytron
  - Videoalvo (VD-850 A)
- Hometronics
  - Telecourt HVG-110
  - Telecourt HVG-220
- Honeybell
  - Video-Sports Color (Honeybell-55)
- IMC
  - Colorgame
- Ingersoll
  - TV Game R-1800
- Ingersoll
  - XK 410C, Multi-colour Sport
- Intercord
  - Color Tank-TV-Spiel (CTVS 11)
  - TVS-4 Electronic
- INTerELektronik
  - Super-Telesport (D-688/36)
  - TV Sport 1004 (D-670/37)
  - TV Sport 3006 (D-713/36)
  - TV-Super Sport 1006
- Interstate Electronics Ltd.
  - Colour Pistol TV Game (1165)
  - Mini TV Game (1102)
  - Mini TV Game (1104)
  - Multisport TV Game (1110)
  - Pistol TV Game-1160
  - Programaster 1125
  - TVG-1199

- Interton
  - Club Exclusiv 2000
  - Video 2400
  - Video 2501
  - Video 2800
  - Video 3001
- ITMC
  - Telejeu 6 jeux SD 017F
- ITT
  - Ideal Computer Tele-Match Cassette 1
- Kind 4 Video Computer Games
  - TV 003
- Kiyo-Seiwa
  - Color Video Attack S-560C
  - Color Video Game (CS? 700)
  - Electronic Action TV Game Model 200
  - Kodak Color Film
  - Video Attack 7
  - Video Attack TG-7800
  - Video Sports (SG-1000)
- Koninklijke Philips NV
  - Odyssey 2001
  - Tele-Spiel ES 2203 Las Vegas
  - Tele-Spiel ES 2204
  - Tele-Spiel ES 2207 Travemünde
  - Videojeu N20
  - Videojeu N30
- Körting Radio Werke
  - Tele-Multi Play (825/042)
  - Tele-Multiplay 4000 (825-301)
  - Tele-Multiplay 6000 (825-328)
  - Tele-Multiplay L (825-050)
- Lark
  - TG-621
- Leaphon
  - Tele-Jeux TJ-140
- Lloyd's
  - TV-Sports 802 (mod.802)
  - TV-Sports 813 (mod.813)

- Magnavox
  - Odyssey 2000
  - Odyssey 3000
  - Odyssey 4000
- Maree Electrónica
  - Video Pinball
- Markint
  - 304 Video Game
  - 4A Video Game
  - 6 (96)
  - T1 Tank Heroique
  - Tele-Sports
  - TV Sport 2002
  - TV-Sport 2001
  - TV-Sport 6002
- Match
  - Match Color (NTL 600)
  - SD-01
  - Spectrum 6, Color-fernsehspiel
- MBO
  - Tele-Ball
  - Tele-Ball II
  - Tele-Ball III
  - Tele-Ball IV
  - Tele-Ball V
  - Tele-Ball VI
  - Tele-Ball VII
  - Teleball-Cassetten-System
  - TG-621
- Mentor
  - Colour 10 TV Game
  - Colour 6 TV Game
  - Colour TV Game
  - Sport TG 20
  - Tele-Sports
- Mercury
  - Commander
- Miragame
  - GM-402
- Montgomery Ward Video
  - World Of Sports
- Music Leader
  - Multi-Play 3300
- Mustang
  - 9008
  - 9009 Video game
  - 9012 Color video game
  - 9014 Panzerschlacht
  - 9015

- Neutron
  - NV1001
  - NV404 video game
- Nintendo
  - Color TV-Game 15
  - Color TV-Game 6
- Norda
  - Colour TV Game H-906
  - TV Game H-915
  - TV Game H-925
  - TV Game TG-621
- Novex
  - Colour Video Sports Game TV 9006
  - TV game TV-9010-C
  - TV-9005
- Novoton
  - TJ-141
  - video sports (TJ-142)
- OPL
  - Optim Sport (Mark I)
  - Optim TV Sport TVG-203
  - Optim TV4+ Four-Way Video Game
- Otron
  - Gamatic 7600
  - Gamatic 7704
  - Gamatic 7706

- Palladium
  - Polygame Tele-Match
  - Tele-Match (825-182)
  - Tele-Match (825-425)
  - Tele-Match (825-468)
  - Tele-Match 4000 (825-131)
  - Tele-Match 6000 (825-166)
  - Tele-Match Color (825-344)
  - Tele-Match Color (825-452)
  - Tele-Match Color (825-484)
  - Tele-Match Color R (825-352)
  - Tele-Match R (825-387)
  - Tele-Multiplay SR (825-417)
- Palson
  - CX-302
  - CX-303
  - CX-306 Super 10 Color
  - CX-340
- Panoramic
  - Telematch (J5)
  - Telematch Junior
  - Telematch Nuclear
- Pathé-Marconi
  - Jeu Video JV1V
  - Jeu Video JV2V
  - Jeu Video JV402V
  - Jeu Video JV602V
- Philco
  - Telejogo
- Phone-Mate inc.
  - Zonk
- Polycon
  - 4002
  - 4003
- Poppy
  - Tele-spiel 9009
- Prim
  - 6 Video Jeux TV

- Prinztronic
  - Micro 10
  - Tournament 6 Colour TV Game
  - Tournament Colour Programmable TV Game 2000
  - Tournament II De Luxe
  - Tournament III (de luxe) - colour electronic TV game
  - Tournament Mini
- QuadTronics
  - Electronic Color TV Game Q-376
  - Electronic Color TV Game Q-476
- R10
  - 9012
  - Telespiel 9010
- Radiola
  - Jeu electronic televise T-02
  - Jeu electronic televise T-03
- RadioShack
  - TV Scoreboard 60-3055
  - TV Scoreboard 60-3056
  - TV Scoreboard 60-3057
  - TV Scoreboard 60-3060
  - TV Scoreboard 60-3061
- Radofin
  - K-Mart SC Eight Thousand (SC8000)
  - K-Mart TV Electronic S Four Thousand S4000
  - Tele-Sports (Black and White)
  - Tele-sports mini
- Re-El
  - Giochi TV 400
  - Giochi TV 402
  - Giochi TV4 401
  - Giochi TV6 403
- Regent
  - TV game (t-338/au-807)

- Ricochet Electronics
  - 8 Electronic TV Game (MT-1A8)
  - Super Pro (MT-4A)
- Ridgewood
  - Gamatic 7600
- Riva
  - T-800
- Roberts
  - Rally IV
  - Rally X
  - Sportrama 8 (36)
  - Super Color Video X
  - Super Color Volley X
  - Volley VI
- Rollet
  - Video Secam System 4-303
- Ronex
  - TV Game Centre (15)
  - TV-Spill - 2 pistols Colour
- Salora
  - Playmaster
- Samdo
  - GM-402
- Sands TM
  - Color TV Game C-2500 UHF
  - Colour TV Game C-2300
  - TV Game C-2200
  - TV Game C-3000
- Santron
  - Home T.V. Game TG-101
- Sanwa
  - 9012 Color Video Game
  - 9015 Color-Cassetten
  - Tele-spiel 9009

- Sears Tele-Games
  - Hockey-Jokari
  - Hockey-Tennis (99722)
  - Hockey-Tennis II (99733)
  - Hockey-Tennis III (99734)
  - Motocross Sports Center IV (99729)
  - Pinball Breakaway (99713)
  - Pong Sports II (99707)
  - Pong Sports IV (99708)
  - Super Pong IV (99789)
- Sennheiser
  - TV Game TVG-96 Coleur
- Sheen
  - 4711 Most Exciting Tank Battle
  - Color TV Sports TVG-406-6
  - Colour Video Sport 106C
  - TVG-201
  - TVG-468-10
  - Video Game TVG-202
  - Video Sport 104
  - Video-Sport 100
- Siemens
  - Bildmeister Turnier FZ 2001
- Silcom
  - Telegioco
- Silora
  - Telegame 2001
- Single IC
  - VG-8-C
- Skylark
  - Video Sport 124
- Société occitane d'électronique
  - Match Junior/Robot - Occitel 2
  - Occitel 003 Modular TV Game
- Sonico
  - 406-6 Color TV Sports Video Game

- Sonnesta
  - Hide-away TV Game
- Sonolor
  - Telematch
- Soundic
  - SD-04 TV Sports B&W
  - SD-04 TV Sports colour
  - Video game SD-01 (TV sport)
  - Video Raceway
- Sportel
  - NTL-600 Video TV Game
  - XY-4
- Sportron
  - 101
  - 105
  - 201
- Super Raf
  - TVG-621
- Superlectron
  - TV Challenger Series 3000 (TVC-3000)
- Syrelec
  - Videoshoot
  - Videoshoot 2
- TAE (Técnicas Avanzadas Electrónicas)
  - Varius-Play
- Takatoku Toys
  - T.U.G.
  - Video Cassette Rock
- Talent
  - Talent TV & Pong set
- Tandy Corporation
  - TV Scoreboard 60-3060
  - TV Scoreboard 60-3061
  - TV Scoreboard 60-9001
  - TV Scoreboard 60-9005
- TCR
  - Video Sport 600
  - Video Sport 7701
- TEC
  - FS-204 Fernsehspiel
  - FS4 Fernsehspiel
  - FS-404

- Technigraph
  - TV Sport
  - TV Sport mark I
  - TVG SD-1
- Teleflip
  - Paris Video Sport FY-707
- Telegioca
  - Match I
- Telegol
  - Telegol
  - Telegol 2
- Teleigra
  - Palestra 02
- Tele-Match inc.
  - Tele Match 4 (model 7700)
  - Tele-Match 4 (6600)
  - Television Computer Game 3300R
- Teleng
  - Colourstars
  - Colourstars TV game
  - Telestars
- Tele-Partner
  - Giochi Televisivi (BN-606P)
  - Giochi Televisivi (Mod. G)
  - TVG-SD-04
  - Video Game Tank-Battle - SD-02-3
- Teleplay
  - TV Games
- Temco
  - T106C
  - T-802
  - T-802C
- Termbray
  - TV Game
  - Video Game TVG-204
- Thomson
  - Jeu Video JV 1T
  - Jeu Video JV 402T
  - JV 1002
- Tokyo
  - Colour 4
  - Colour 6

- Tomy
  - TV Fun 301
  - TV Fun 401
  - TV Fun Color Model 501
  - TV Fun Color Model 601
  - TV Fun Color Model 602
  - TV Fun Color Model 701
- Toshiba
  - Video Game TVG-610
- Trensi
  - Color TV Sports TVG-406-6
- TRQ Talleres Radioeléctricos Querol
  - S.L. Tele Juego - B/N 4
- TRQ - Talleres Radioeléctricos Querol
  - S.L. Tele-Juego Color-4
- Ultrasound
  - Tele-Sports
  - TV-9010
  - TV-9010-C
- Unimex
  - Mark III
  - Mark IV
  - Mark V
  - Mark VI
  - Mark VII
  - Mark VIII
- Unisonic Products Corporation
  - Olympian 2600
  - Tournament 1000
  - Tournament 2000
  - Tournament 2501
- Unitrex
  - Video Action
  - Video-Pro
  - Video-Pro II
- Universum
  - Color-Multi-Spiel 4004
  - TV-Multi Spiel 2004
- Univox
  - 41N
  - 4200n

- Vanica
  - TV game AU-708
- Venture Electronics
  - Video Sports VS-5
  - Video Sports VS-7
- Video
  - 4000-EX DX-503
  - Stellar 5 Jeux - 2002
- Videomaster
  - Colourscore (VM11)
  - Colourshot (VMV2)
  - Strika (VM-13)
  - Strika 2 (VMV8)
  - Visionscore (VMV1)
- Videoton
  - Sportron 101
- Waltham
  - W TV-4
- Weiner
  - WG-015
- Windsor
  - TV Game EP460
- Winthronics
  - Video Game D-5614
- Y.S.A.
  - Sport King Model-103
  - TV Sports Star Model-105
- Yoko
  - Sportfun TV game
- Zanussi
  - Play-O-Tronic
- Zeon
  - T-338
  - T-800
  - t-800c
- Zhoushi Electronic Enterprise Co., Ltd.
  - Zoushi TV

1978

- Acetronic
  - Colour TV Game
  - Tele-Sports IV
- Akur
  - Video SD-050
- Alltronic
  - 7000 Color

- Audiosonic
  - Most Exciting Home Video Game TVG-201 (TVG 201-4)
- PP-150
- PP-790
- PP-795
- PP-920 (920B)
- PP-920C
- PP-920D
- PP-930
- PP-940
- Programmable tele-sports III
- Tele-Sports IV
- Tele-Sports Mini
- TVG-4
- TVG-6 Color tv game
- Bandai Co., Ltd.
  - TV JACK 5000
- Binatone
  - Cablestar (01-4362)
  - Colour TV Game (01-4931)
  - Colour TV Game 4 plus 2 (01-4850)
  - Colour TV Game MK 10 (01-4842)
  - Colour TV Game MK 6 (01-4761)
  - Superstar (01-4354)
- BMC
  - Video Game TVG-8000 Champion 77
- Coleco
  - Telstar Colortron
  - Telstar Gemini
  - Telstar Marksman
  - Telstar Sportsman
- Concord
  - Programmable TV Game 501
- Creatronic
  - Bi.Bip 100
  - Program 2000 SD-05

- Dick Smith
  - Programmable TV Game Console Y-1160
  - Video Ball Game Kit
- Electronic Do Brasil
  - TV Bol
- Electronika
  - Eksi-Video 01
- Electrosport
  - Colour T.V. Games TV 01
- Eletron
  - Tv-Jogo Canal 14
- Elwro PPZ Ameprod
  - Ameprod Television Game 10
- Epoch Co.
  - TV Baseball
- Glorytone
  - Video Olympiad Colorama (7701)
- Granada Electronics
  - Colorsport VIII (CS1818)
- Grandstand
  - Colour Cartridge SD050
  - Colour Programmable SD070
- Grundig
  - Tele-Spiel 1
- Hanimex
  - 666
  - 677
  - Programmable TV-game TVG-050C
  - SD-070 Colour (programmable TV-game console)
  - TVG 3000
- Harvard
  - Color TV game (H-11)
  - H-1
  - H-5 Mini Color TV Game
- HGS Electronic
  - Telesport Model 4

- Hobbytron
  - Videorama
- Ingersoll
  - Battle Command XK-1010
  - Colour Match XK-500C
  - Programmable Video Console XK-4000
  - Tele-sports mini TV Game (XK 400)
  - XK 600B screenplay
- Intercord
  - Telespiel TVS-6
  - TV Games TVS-5
- INTerELektronik GmbH (Intel)
  - Grand Prix (D-731/07)
  - Monza (D-719/00)
  - TV Sport 2004
  - TV Sport 4010
  - TV Sport 5010 (Art.D759/36)
- Irradio
  - TVG-888
- ITT Schaub-Lorenz
  - Ideal Computer Tele-Match Cassette 2
  - Ideal Computer Tele-Match Cassette 3
  - Ideal Computer Tele-Match Cassette 4
- Klervox
  - Jeu TV TVG-6
  - SD-050S color
  - TV Sports - TVG SD-04
  - TVG-621
- Koninklijke Philips NV
  - Odyssey 2100
  - Tele-Spiel ES 2208 Las Vegas super color
  - Tele-Spiel ES 2218 Las Vegas
- Körting Radio Werke
  - Tele-Multiplay 8000 (825-336)

- Lark
  - Programmable TV Game - TVG-868
  - TV Sport
- Lasonic
  - 2000 T.V. Game
- Logitec
  - Color TV Game CT-7600CG
- Mach
  - SD-05
- Malitron
  - TV Jogo 10
- Maree Electrónica
  - Video Pinball-10
- Match
  - Match Color (AY-3-8610)
- MBO
  - Tele-Ball IX
  - Tele-Ball VIII (0443)
  - Teleball-Cassetten-System II
- Mercury
  - Commander Mark III
- Monarch
  - CTX-2000 programmable video computer
  - Video Sporter
  - Video Sporter CTX-4 Color
  - Video Sporter GXL-4
  - Video Sporter XTL-4
- Nintendo
  - Color TV Game Racing 112
- Novex
  - Computerized Electronic Programmable Video Game 1010
- Olympos
  - Electronic Gamatic 7600
  - Electronic Gamatic 7706
- OPL
  - Optim 600 colour

- Palladium
  - Tele-Cassetten-Game Color (825-530)
  - Tele-Cassetten-Game Color (825-581)
- Phonola
  - Teleflipper
- Polistil
  - Video Games V.G.2
- Polycon
  - C-4010
  - PG-7 Programmable TV Games
- Poppy
  - TV-Game Fernseh Spiel TVG-4
- Prinztronic
  - Grandprix
  - Micro 5500
  - Tournament Colour Programmable 5000
  - Videosport 600 - Electronic TV Game
  - Videosport 800 - colour electronic tv game
- Radofin
  - tele-sports III
- Rollet
  - Robot 4302
  - Robot OC 5000
- S.H.G.
  - Black Point 10 - Tele Sports FS 1002
  - Black Point FS 1003
  - Black Point FS 2000
  - Black Point Multicolor FS 1001
- Saft Groupe S.A.
  - TV8 Sports
- Sands
  - TM Color TV Game C-2600

- Schneider Electric
  - Télélude
  - Telelude NB2
- Scomark
  - 10 Sports Tele
  - 4 Sports Tele
  - 8 Sports Tele
  - jeu tv TVG-6
- Sears Tele-Games
  - 80007
  - Gunslinger II
  - Speedway (80017)
  - Speedway IV (99748)
  - Speedway S-100 (99747)
- Sheen
  - 9015
- Sinoca
  - T.V. Game
- Sipo
  - TV Spiel Color SD-050
- Société occitane d'électronique
  - OC 5000
- Soundic
  - Programmable TV-Game Console SD-050 / SD-05 / SD-050S
  - Programmable TV-Game Console SD-090
  - SD-023C Tank Battle
  - SD-062 TV-18
  - SD-61
  - TV-game programmable SD-070C Sport
- Soviet Union
  - Eureka (Эврика)
  - Turnir
- Sportron
  - 108
  - Programaster
- Starex
  - Jeux video 501
  - Jeux video 502

- TCR
  - Video Sport 7705
  - Video Sport 7801 (104)
  - Video Sport 900 Programmable
  - Cartridge game in color
- Tele-Partner
  - TV Game Programmable (CL-2002)
- Teleplay
  - Colour Programagame
  - Grand Prix
  - Video Entertainment Unit
- Tempest
  - Programmable TVGame SD-050C
- Tomy
  - TV Fun 801
  - Tv Fun 901
  - TV Fun Color Model 902
- TV18 (TV 2018)
  - TV 18 Color (C-4016)
  - TV 2018 Color (20 441/2)
- Unimex
  - TV-10 Color (Mark IX)
- Unimor
  - TELE-SET GTV 881
- Universum
  - TV-Multi-spiel 2006
- Uni-Vid
  - F-8 (703 SE)
- Univox
  - 6IN
  - Jeu Video Cassette Tele-sports III
- Video
  - Stellar Combat Lunaire
- Videomaster
  - All Star (VMV9)
- Sportsworld (VMV5)

1979

- Duette
  - Color C4016 Video Games
- Epoch Co.
  - TV Block
- Grandstand Sports
  - Centre 5000 Colour
  - TVG-3600 1/MKII/MKIII
- Hanimex
  - T-338
- INTerELektronik GmbH (Intel)
  - Universal Tele-Play (D-744/34)
- JostyKit
  - Multi-TV-Game HF344
- Magiclick
  - Teleclick
- Nintendo
  - Color TV Game Block Breaker
- Philco
  - Telejogo II
- Polycon
  - C-4016
- Prinztronic
  - Tournament Ten - Colour de luxe video TV game
- Sixplay
  - Sixplay
- Société occitane d'électronique
  - OC 6000
  - OC 7000 Bataille de Tanks
- Temco
  - T-800
  - T-800C
  - T900
- Universum
  - Color-Multi-Spiel 4010
- Videomaster
  - Colour Cartridge (VMV12)
  - Colourscore 2 (VMV6)

1980

- Epoch Co.
  - TV Vader

- Grandstand
  - Sports Centre 6000
- Halbleiterwerk
  - Frankfurt (Oder) Kombinat Mikroelektronik Erfurt BSS 01
- Nintendo
  - Computer TVgame
- Nordmende
  - Color TelePlay
- TRQ - Talleres Radioeléctricos Querol
  - S.L. Tele-Juego Color-10
- Universum
  - TV-Multi-Spiel 4014

1981

- Electronika
  - ideosport
- Radofin
  - Colour TV Game (Telesports)
  - Tele-sports IV
- Soviet Union
  - BTSTI + Rubin Ts1-205
- Universum
  - Color Multi-Spiel 4106
- Univox
  - Telesport 10
  - Tele-Sports 6

1982

- Audiosonic
  - Color TV Game PP-160
- Intercord
  - Tele-Computer XL-2000
- ITMC
  - Telejeu SD-043
- Miragame
  - Color Game GMC-802
- Poppy
  - Colour Video Game 9012

1983

- Bentley Industries inc
  - . Compu-Vision 440
- DMS - Clayton Group Ltd.
  - Tele-Action mini GMT513
  - Tele-Sports Mini
- Electronika
  - Videosport 3
- J. C. Penney
  - Video Sports - Electronic 4-in-1

1993

- Electronika
  - Leader

Other Consoles

- Ajax
  - T-338
  - TVG-621
- Alfa Electronics PTE. LTD.
  - Videotronic
  - Videotronic II (3388)
  - Videotronic II (8550C)
- APF Electronics, Inc.
  - V Fun 444
- Asaki
  - TVG 200
  - TVG-209-4
- Atari, Inc.
  - Hockey Pong
  - Pong Doubles
  - Stunt Cycle (C-450)
  - Super Pong (C-140)
  - Super Pong PRO-AM (C-200)
  - Super Pong PRO-AM Ten (C-202)
  - Super Pong Ten (C-180)
  - Pong (C-402 S)
  - Ultra Pong Doubles

- Boyang Electronic corporation
  - Colormate de Luxe
- CAM
  - TVG-872
- Consolidate Enterprises
  - Convoy 7706
- Delta
  - Delta III Videogame
- Electronika
  - Eksi-Video 02
  - Videosport-2
  - Videosport-M
- Entex Industries
  - Gameroom Tele-Pong (3047)
- ERS: Electronic Readout Systems inc.
  - Mod.2
- Farad Electronics PTY LDT.
  - T.V. Sport / Video Action
- Federal
  - 7620
- Friwo Gerätebau GmbH
  - TV-Sport GX4
- Grandstand
  - TV Game Adman 2000
- Hanimex
  - TVG 070C
  - TVG-8610
  - TVG-8610C
- Híradástechnikai Szövetkezet
  - TV games
- Hit-Go
  - HIT-10

- Inno-Hit
  - GT-10C
  - GT-16C
  - GT-20C
  - GT-4N (Sportron)
  - GT-66C
  - GT-6N
- ITMC
  - SD 90
  - SD-040F
  - SD-050
- Jet Signal Industries CO.
  - T.V. Game
- Laboratorio Electrónico
  - Hiroshima Videojuel
- Lloyd's
  - TV Sports 812
- Luxor Systems
  - Sportsman 2001
- Noblex Argentina
  - Micro 14 14NT320
- Novedades Electronicas
  - S.A. Nesa Pong
- OPL
  - Optim Sport T-338
- Otron
  - Gamatic 8600 Programmable Video Game
- Palson
  - CX-336 Game Cassette System
- Poppy
  - 9017 Colour TV Game
  - 9015
  - TVG-10
  - TVG-3

- Prinztronic
  - Tournament IV
- Rado Sonic
  - Most Exciting Home Video Game
  - TV games
- Radofin
  - Electronic TV Game Tele-sport 10 (color)
  - Jeux video 3011
  - Sport-Action TV Game
- Sears Tele-Games
  - Super Pong (99736)
- Sipo
  - C-2600 Colour
- Soundic
  - TV Sport
- Sportel Paddle IV
- TD Manufacturing Co.
  - Video Volley
- Teleflip
  - Paris Video Couleur CB-812
- Tenko
  - TV Game (PP-150 Giocattolo)
- Tokyo
  - Colour 10
- Trevi s.r.l.
  - Color TV Sport 406-6
- Universum
  - TV-Spiel 1004
- Verco
  - TV Spel T-338

SECOND GENERATION

1976-1992

Gerry Lawson

In the mid-1970s, engineer Gerry Lawson worked at Fairchild Semiconductor, a company known for its pioneering work in the semiconductor industry.

During his time at Fairchild Semiconductor, Lawson was involved in various engineering projects related to integrated circuits and semiconductor technology. His expertise in semiconductor engineering and electronics contributed to the company's overall advancements in microprocessor technology.

Microprocessors are central processing units (CPUs) contained on a single integrated circuit, and they serve as the "brain" of a computer or electronic device. Fairchild Semiconductor played a crucial role in the early development of microprocessors, with some of its engineers and researchers making significant contributions to this technology.

Lawson and his team at Fairchild were tasked with creating a home gaming console that could surpass the limitations of earlier dedicated consoles and offer players a more diverse and expandable gaming experience.

In 1976, the team, led by Lawson, successfully launched the Fairchild Channel F. This console was the first to feature interchangeable game cartridges, allowing players to access different games by simply inserting a new cartridge into the console. This innovation revolutionized the gaming industry, as it provided a vast library of games without the need for separate dedicated hardware for each title.

The Fairchild Channel F featured more advanced graphics and sound capabilities compared to its predecessors, adding to the appeal of home gaming. Gerry Lawson's work played a crucial role in shaping the trajectory of the video game industry.

Atari's Acquisition

As Atari grew rapidly, it transitioned from a small start-up to a larger corporation. With this growth came the introduction of a more traditional corporate structure and management. Nolan Bushnell, known for his entrepreneurial and innovative spirit, clashed with the corporate management style, which led to disagreements over the direction of the company.

In 1976, Warner Communications (now WarnerMedia) acquired Atari. The new ownership brought changes to the company's structure and decision-making processes, which may have been at odds with Bushnell's vision and approach to business.

The Atari VCS/2600

The Atari 2600, released in 1977 as the Atari Video Computer System (VCS), is a landmark home video game console that left a significant mark on the history of gaming. Developed by Atari, Inc., it was a key player in the second generation of gaming and popularized the concept of interchangeable game cartridges.

The Atari 2600 introduced a new era of gaming with its innovative cartridge-based system. Players could expand their gaming library by simply inserting different game cartridges, providing a diverse range of gaming experiences without the need for separate dedicated hardware.

The console's joystick controller became iconic and synonymous with video gaming. With its single-button design, the joystick provided an intuitive way for players to interact with games.

Despite its relatively simple graphics and sound capabilities compared to modern standards, the Atari 2600's games were revolutionary for their time. Titles like "Pac-Man," "Space Invaders," and "Asteroids" became classics that are still celebrated today.

Technical Enhancements

The second generation marked the rise of home gaming consoles as a dominant force in the industry. Companies like Atari, Mattel, Coleco, and Intellivision released popular gaming systems designed for home use.

Unlike the first generation's dedicated consoles, the second generation introduced cartridge-based systems like the Atari 2600, Intellivision, and ColecoVision. This allowed players to swap out cartridges to play different games, providing a vast library of titles.

Technical enhancements brought significant improvements in graphics compared to the simple visuals of the first generation. Games featured more detailed and colourful graphics, enhancing the gaming experience. Sound capabilities were also significantly enhanced, with games featured more complex audio effects and background music, adding to the immersion of gameplay.

The second generation saw the emergence of various game genres, including action, adventure, sports, and more. Developers explored different themes and gameplay mechanics, offering players a broader range of gaming experiences.

Many arcade games from the first generation were successfully ported to second-generation consoles. Players could now enjoy arcade classics like Space Invaders, Pac-Man, and Donkey Kong in their own homes.

Bushnell's Exit

As Atari expanded and diversified, there were differing opinions on the future of the company and its product lineup. Nolan Bushnell's focus was on pushing the boundaries of gaming and creating innovative experiences, while the corporate management may have been more concerned with profitability and market stability.

Atari faced financial challenges and rapid expansion, including ventures into various industries beyond video games. These financial pressures may have led to differing priorities between Bushnell and the corporate leadership, and it is believed Bushnell's vision for the future of Atari and his entrepreneurial ambitions may not have aligned with the long-term plans of the corporate owners.

Due to these various factors, Nolan Bushnell resigned from Atari in 1978. He went on to explore other entrepreneurial ventures, including founding the Chuck E. Cheese's pizza and entertainment restaurant chain, which combined dining with arcade gaming.

Activision and Third-Party video games

Activision was formed in 1979 as a result of a unique situation involving a group of disgruntled game developers at Atari, Inc. The key figures involved in the formation of Activision were David Crane, Larry Kaplan, Alan Miller, and Bob Whitehead, all of whom were talented game programmers at Atari.

During their time at Atari, these developers were responsible for creating some of the company's most successful and innovative games. However, they became dissatisfied with Atari's corporate structure and the lack of recognition and compensation for their work. Atari had a policy at the time that did not credit developers on the game boxes, which led to them feeling undervalued.

In a groundbreaking move, these developers decided to leave Atari and form their own independent game development company, where they could have more creative freedom and receive proper recognition for their work. On October 1, 1979, they founded Activision, becoming the first third-party video game developer.

One of the crucial aspects of Activision's formation was the legal challenge they posed to Atari's policy on crediting developers. The case centred around Activision's right to develop and publish games for the Atari 2600 console, despite Atari's attempt to prevent them from doing so.

Atari argued that they held exclusive rights to produce games for their own console, and third-party developers like Activision were violating those rights.

Activision contended that their games were entirely original creations, and they were not using any copyrighted or patented materials from Atari's games. They argued that the games they developed were their own intellectual property and did not infringe on Atari's rights.

The court case went to trial, and in 1982, the court ruled in favour of Activision. The judge's decision upheld the legitimacy of third-party game developers and their right to create and publish games for the Atari 2600 console. The ruling set a precedent for the video game industry, paving the way for other third-party developers to enter the market and offer their own games for various gaming platforms.

With the legal battle behind them, Activision began creating and publishing games for various gaming platforms, including the Atari 2600. Their early titles, such as "Pitfall!" and "River Raid," were highly successful and helped establish the company as a major player in the industry.

The Introduction of Handhelds

The second generation in the late 1970s and early 1980s saw the emergence of handheld games consoles, marking the inception of portable gaming and laying the groundwork for the thriving industry we know today. These pioneering devices, though rudimentary by today's standards, captured the imaginations of players and set the stage for the evolution of handheld gaming.

One of the most influential handheld consoles (and considered by many to be the first true handheld) was the Milton Bradley Microvision, launched in 1979. It was the first handheld console to feature interchangeable cartridges, allowing players to enjoy different games on a single device. Despite its limited success, the Microvision laid the foundation for future handheld consoles by introducing the concept of expandable gaming libraries.

In 1980, Nintendo made its entry into the handheld gaming market with the release of the Game & Watch series. These devices, designed by Gunpei Yokoi, featured LCD screens and dedicated games pre-programmed into each unit. The Game & Watch series achieved immense popularity, selling millions of units and establishing Nintendo as a major player in the gaming industry.

Other notable handheld consoles of this generation included the Entex Adventure Vision, which offered a unique 3D gaming experience, and the Select-A-Game. These devices showcased the early experimentation with different gameplay mechanics and features in the handheld gaming landscape.

This generation of handheld games consoles faced limitations in terms of graphics, sound capabilities, and game variety. However, their novelty, convenience, and the thrill of gaming on the go captivated players and set the stage for further advancements in portable gaming technology.

The first "Console War"

The first console war refers to the intense competition and rivalry between two major video game companies during the early 1980s: Atari and Mattel.

Atari, with its successful Atari 2600 console, had already established itself as a dominant player in the video game market. However, Mattel Electronics, a division of the toy company Mattel, decided to challenge Atari's position by releasing their own gaming console, the Intellivision.

The Intellivision, released in 1979, was a technically advanced console compared to the Atari 2600. It boasted improved graphics and sound capabilities, offering a more sophisticated gaming experience. The console's slogan, "Intelligent Television," emphasized its superior technology over the Atari 2600.

The launch of the Intellivision intensified the competition between Atari and Mattel. Both companies engaged in aggressive marketing campaigns to attract consumers to their respective consoles. They sought to convince players that their system offered the best gaming experience and the most diverse library of games.

The battle for market dominance between Atari and Mattel during the early 1980s marked the first major console war in the video game industry. The competition led to a surge in innovation as both companies worked to outdo each other, resulting in a flurry of new games and technological advancements. Although the Intellivision enjoyed relative success, the Atari 2600 remained the best-selling console of the generation.

The 1983 Video Game Crash and the downfall of the Second Generation

The video game crash was a significant downturn in the video game industry that occurred in North America during the early 1980s. It was characterized by a sudden and severe decline in video game sales, resulting in the near-collapse of the home video game market.

In the late 1970s and early 1980s, the video game industry experienced explosive growth, leading to an oversaturation of the market with numerous consoles and games. The market became flooded with low-quality games and shovelware, resulting in consumer confusion and dissatisfaction.

With the rise of third-party game developers, many low-quality games were rushed to market without proper testing and development. These subpar games led to a loss of consumer confidence in the industry.

The fierce competition between gaming companies led to price wars and a race to the bottom in terms of pricing. This, coupled with declining game quality, negatively impacted revenue for developers and publishers.

The rise in popularity of home computers, like the Commodore 64 and the Apple II, offered more versatile and sophisticated gaming experiences, drawing attention away from dedicated gaming consoles.

As a result of these factors, video game sales plummeted, leading to massive financial losses for gaming companies and retailers. Many companies went bankrupt, and retailers faced substantial unsold inventory. Atari even went as far as to bury huge quantities of unsold stock in a New Mexico landfill site.

Home Consoles

☐Fairchild Channel F

RELEASE DATE	USA: November 1976
	JP: October 1977
DISCONTINUED	1983
ORIGINAL PRICE	$169.95
UNITS SOLD	Approx. 350,000
BEST-SELLING GAME	Videocart-17 Pinball Challenge

The Fairchild Channel F, released in 1976, holds a significant place in the history of video gaming as one of the earliest programmable cartridge-based video game consoles. Developed by Fairchild Semiconductor, this innovative console marked a crucial milestone in the evolution of home video gaming.

The Fairchild Channel F was the brainchild of Jerry Lawson, an engineer at Fairchild Semiconductor. The goal was to create a gaming system that offered players more flexibility and variety in their gaming experiences. Unlike its predecessors, which featured built-in games with fixed gameplay, the Channel F allowed users to switch games through interchangeable cartridges. This groundbreaking concept set the stage for the future of gaming, where players could access a wide array of titles without the need for separate dedicated consoles.

The console's design was relatively simple, featuring a compact and sleek appearance. It came with two detachable controllers that resembled rectangular joysticks with a single red button. The Channel F connected to the television set through the antenna input, and players could enjoy their games in black and white or color, depending on their TV's capabilities.

The Fairchild Channel F featured a series of innovative games, many of which are now considered classics. Titles like "Video Whizball," "Space War," and "Robot War/Torpedo Alley" offered players engaging and entertaining experiences, despite the console's technical limitations.

In terms of hardware, the Fairchild Channel F utilized the Fairchild F8 microprocessor, which was one of the first commercially available microprocessors used in a gaming console. Although its processing power and graphics were limited compared to modern systems, the Channel F's capabilities were groundbreaking for its time.

One of the Channel F's unique features was its "Channel Guard" switch, which allowed players to alter certain aspects of the game, such as changing the difficulty level or the number of players. This provided an early form of game customization that added to the console's appeal.

Despite its innovations and forward-thinking design, the Fairchild Channel F faced stiff competition from the more popular and better-marketed Atari 2600, which was released a year later. The Atari 2600's marketing prowess and extensive library of games gave it a competitive advantage in the emerging console market.

While the Fairchild Channel F did not achieve the same commercial success as some of its competitors, its contributions to the gaming industry should not be overlooked. Its pioneering concept of cartridge-based gaming laid the groundwork for subsequent gaming consoles, and its games continue to be remembered fondly by gaming enthusiasts and historians.

Games List

- Chess (integrated)
- Hockey (integrated)
- Tennis (integrated)
- Videocart-1: Tic-Tac-Toe, Shooting Gallery, Doodle, Quadra-Doodle
- Videocart-2: Desert Fox, Shooting Gallery
- Videocart-3: Video Blackjack
- Videocart-4: Spitfire
- Videocart-5: Space War
- Videocart-6: Math Quiz I (Addition & Subtraction)
- Videocart-7: Math Quiz II (Multiplication & Division)
- Videocart-8: Magic Numbers (Mind Reader & Nim)
- Videocart-9: Drag Race
- Videocart-10: Maze, Jailbreak, Blind-Man's-Bluff, Trailblazer
- Videocart-11: Backgammon, Acey-Deucey
- Videocart-11: Backgammon, Acey-Deucey
- Videocart-12: Baseball
- Videocart-13: Robot War, Torpedo Alley
- Videocart-14: Sonar Search
- Videocart-15: Memory Match 1, Memory Match
- Videocart-16: Dodge' It
- Videocart-17: Pinball Challenge
- Videocart-18: Hangman
- Videocart-19: Checkers
- Videocart-20: Video Whizball
- Videocart-21: Bowling
- Videocart-22: Slot Machine
- Videocart-23: Galactic Space Wars
- Videocart-24: Pro Football
- Videocart-25: Casino Poker
- Videocart-26: Alien Invasion

□RCA Studio II

RELEASE DATE	January 1977
DISCONTINUED	1978
ORIGINAL PRICE	$149
UNITS SOLD	53,000-64,000
BEST-SELLING GAME	N/A

The RCA Studio II is a lesser-known but historically significant video game console that holds a unique place in the early history of home gaming. Developed by RCA Corporation, the Studio II was among the first consoles to offer programmable games, marking a notable step forward in the evolution of video gaming.

The RCA Studio II was introduced as a successor to the original RCA Studio I, which was a dedicated console offering simple built-in games. However, the Studio I lacked the versatility and expandability that players were beginning to seek in their gaming experiences. The Studio II aimed to address this limitation by introducing a novel concept - replaceable cartridges.

The console's design was compact and featured a sleek appearance. It connected to the television via an RF adapter, enabling players to access their games on the TV screen. The system came with two attached controllers, each having a numeric keypad and a few action buttons, offering an intuitive yet straightforward gaming experience.

The Studio II's hardware was relatively modest for the time. It featured a custom microprocessor, known as the COSMAC 1802, which also served as a central processing unit in other applications beyond gaming. The console had a limited monochrome display with simple graphics and sound capabilities.

The console's library of games, though small compared to other systems, was one of its standout features. RCA released a series of cartridges that included titles like "Gunfighter/Moonship Battle," "Doodles," and "Bingo Match," offering a variety of gaming experiences to players.

However, the RCA Studio II faced several challenges that impacted its commercial success. One of the main issues was the lack of third-party game development. Unlike its competitors like the Atari 2600, which attracted numerous third-party developers, the Studio II's closed development environment limited the variety and quantity of available games.

The console was released during a time of fierce competition in the emerging home gaming market. The popularity of consoles like the Atari 2600 and the Magnavox Odyssey 2 overshadowed the Studio II, leading to its relatively low sales and limited market presence.

Despite its commercial setbacks, the RCA Studio II remains historically important for its contributions to the early video game industry. It was one of the first consoles to offer replaceable cartridges, providing players with the opportunity to enjoy diverse gaming experiences on a single platform.

Games List

- 18V400|TV Arcade I: Space War
- 18V401|TV Arcade II: Fun with Numbers
- 18V402|TV Arcade III: Tennis/Squash
- 18V403|TV Arcade IV: Baseball
- 18V404|TV Arcade Series: Speedway/Tag
- 18V405|TV Arcade Series: Gunfighter/Moonship Battle
- 18V501|TV School House II: Math Fun
- 18V600|TV Casino I: Blackjack
- 18V601|TV Casino Series: TV Bingo
- 18V700|TV Mystic Series: Biorhythm

☐Atari VCS/Atari 2600

RELEASE DATE	USA: September 1977
	EU: 1978
	JP: May 1983
DISCONTINUED	January 1992
ORIGINAL PRICE	$199
UNITS SOLD	30 million
BEST-SELLING GAME	Pac-Man

The Atari 2600, originally known as the Atari Video Computer System (VCS), is a video game console that holds an iconic place in the history of gaming. Released in 1977 by Atari, Inc., the Atari 2600 was a groundbreaking platform that popularized home video gaming and became a cultural phenomenon.

Atari 2600's design was sleek and futuristic for its time, featuring a wood-grain finish and a distinctive black and brown colour scheme. The console connected to the television via an RF switch, immersing players in the world of gaming on their TV screens.

The Atari 2600's most significant innovation was its use of interchangeable game cartridges. The cartridge-based system allowed players to access a diverse library of games simply by inserting a new cartridge. This revolutionary concept gave players the freedom to choose from a wide range of gaming experiences, making the Atari 2600 an appealing and versatile console.

The console came with a joystick controller, which featured a single red button, providing an intuitive and straightforward way for players to interact with the games. It also had paddle controllers, which allowed for precise control in games like "Pong" and "Breakout."

The Atari 2600's game library featured numerous classics that are still celebrated today. Games like "Space Invaders," "Pac-Man," "Asteroids," and "Pitfall!" became iconic titles that shaped the early gaming experience and remain etched in the memories of gaming enthusiasts.

The console's graphics and sound capabilities were modest compared to modern standards, but they were revolutionary for their time. Players were captivated by the simple yet engaging visuals and the distinctive beeps and bloops that accompanied gameplay.

The Atari 2600's commercial success made it a dominant force in the video game industry during the second generation of gaming. It became a cultural phenomenon and helped define the pop culture of the late 1970s and early 1980s.

However, the Atari 2600's popularity eventually waned due to various factors. The market became oversaturated with low-quality games and competition from other gaming consoles. The North American video game crash of 1983 further impacted the industry, leading to a decline in Atari 2600 sales.

Despite its eventual decline, the Atari 2600's legacy remains firmly intact. It paved the way for subsequent generations of gaming consoles, established the concept of third-party game development and set the stage for the growth and mainstream acceptance of video gaming.

Games List

- 3-D Tic-Tac-Toe
- 32 in 1 (Europe Only)
- Acid Drop
- The Activision Decathlon
- Adventure
- Adventures of Tron
- Air Lock
- Air Raid
- Air Raiders
- Air Sea Battle
- Alien
- Alpha Beam with Ernie
- Amidar
- Arcade Golf
- Arcade Pinball
- Armor Ambush
- Artillery Duel
- Artillery Duel/Chuck Norris Superkicks
- Artillery Duel/Ghost Manor
- Artillery Duel/Spike's Peak
- Assault
- Astérix (Europe Only)
- Asteroids
- Astroblast
- Atari Video Cube
- Atlantis
- Bachelor Party
- Bachelor Party/Gigolo
- Bachelor Party/Burning Desire
- Backgammon
- Bank Heist
- Barnstorming
- Baseball
- Basic Math
- Basic Programming
- Basketball
- Battlezone
- Beamrider
- Beany Bopper
- Beat Em and Eat Em
- Beat Em and Eat Em/Lady in Wadding
- Berenstain Bears
- Bermuda Triangle
- Berzerk
- Big Bird's Egg Catch
- Blackjack
- Blue Print
- BMX Airmaster
- Boing
- Bowling

- Boxing
- Brain Games
- Breakaway IV
- Breakout
- Bridge
- Buck Rogers: Planet of Zoom
- Bugs
- Bump 'n' Jump
- Bumper Bash
- Burgertime
- Busy Police
- Cakewalk
- California Games
- Cannon Man
- Canyon Bomber
- Capture
- Carnival
- Casino
- Centipede
- Challenge
- Challenge of Nexar
- Championship Soccer
- Chase
- Chase the Chuck Wagon
- Checkers
- China Syndrome
- Chopper Command
- Chuck Norris Superkicks
- Chuck Norris Superkicks/Ghost Manor
- Chuck Norris Superkicks/Spike's Peak
- Circus
- Circus Atari
- Coconuts
- Codebreaker
- Combat
- Commando
- Commando Raid
- Concentration
- Condor Attack
- Congo Bongo
- Cookie Monster Munch
- Cosmic Ark
- Cosmic Commuter
- Cosmic Corridor
- Cosmic Creeps
- Cosmic Swarm
- Crackpots
- Crash Dive
- Crazy Climber
- Cross Force
- Crossbow

- Cruise Missile
- Crypts of Chaos
- Crystal Castles
- Custer's Revenge
- Dare Diver
- Dark Cavern
- Dark Chambers
- Deadly Duck
- Death Trap
- Defender
- Defender II
- Demolition Herby
- Demon Attack
- Demons to Diamonds
- Desert Falcon
- Dice Puzzle
- Dig Dug
- Dishaster
- Dodge Em
- Dodger Cars
- Dolphin
- Donkey Kong
- Donkey Kong Jr.
- Double Dragon
- Double Dunk
- Dragonfire
- Dragon Treasure
- Dragster
- Earth Attack
- Earth Dies Screaming
- Eggomania
- Eli's Ladder
- Encounter at L5
- Enduro
- Entombed
- Espial
- E.T. The Extra-Terrestrial
- Exocet
- Fantastic Voyage
- Farmer Dan
- Fast Eddie
- Fast Food
- Fathom
- Final Approach
- Fire Fighter
- Fire Fly
- Fishing Derby
- Flag Capture
- Flash Gordon
- Football
- Football: Real Sports Soccer
- Frankenstein's Monster
- Freeway

- Frogger
- Frogger II: Threeedeep!
- Frogs and Flies
- Front Line
- Frontline
- Frostbite
- Fun with Numbers
- Galaxian
- Gangster Alley
- Gas Hog
- Gauntlet
- Ghost Manor
- Ghost Manor/Spike's Peak
- Ghostbusters
- GI Joe: Cobra Strike
- Glacier Patrol
- Glib
- Golf
- Gopher
- Gorf
- Grand Prix
- Gravitar
- Great Escape
- Gremlins
- Guardian
- Gunslinger
- Gyruss
- Halloween
- Hangman
- Harbor Escape
- Haunted House
- H.E.R.O.
- Home Run
- Human Cannonball
- Hunt & Score
- Ice Hockey
- Ikari Warriors
- Inca Gold
- Indy 500
- Infiltrate
- International Soccer
- I Want My Mommy
- James Bond 007
- Jawbreaker
- Journey Escape
- Joust
- Jr. Pac-Man
- Jungle Fever/Knight on the Town
- Jungle Hunt
- Kaboom!
- Kangaroo
- Karate
- Keystone Kapers
- King Kong
- Kool-Aid Man
- Krull
- Kung Fu Master
- Kung Fu Superkicks
- Laser Blast
- Laser Gates
- Laser Volley
- Lochjaw
- Lock n Chase
- London Blitz
- Lost Luggage
- M.A.D.
- Magicard
- Malagai
- Mangia
- Marauder
- Marine Wars
- Mario Bros.
- M*A*S*H
- Master Builder
- Masters of the Universe: He Man
- Math
- Math Gran Prix
- Maze
- Maze Craze
- Maze Mania
- Mega Force
- Megamania
- Memory Match
- Midnight Magic
- Millipede
- Miner 2049er
- Miner 2049er II
- Mines of Minos
- Miniature Golf
- Missile Command
- Mogul Maniac
- Montezuma's Revenge
- Moon Patrol
- Moonsweeper
- Motocross Racer
- Motorodeo
- Mountain King
- Mouse Trap
- Mr. Do!
- Mr. Do!'s Castle
- Ms. Pac-Man
- Music Machine
- Name This Game
- Night Driver
- No Escape
- Obelix (Europe Only)
- Ocean City Defender
- Off the Wall
- Oink
- Omega Race
- Oscar's Trash Race
- Othello
- Out of Control
- Outer Space
- Outlaw
- Pac-Man
- Pele's Soccer
- Pengo
- Pepsi Invaders
- Pete Rose Baseball
- Philly Flasher/Cathouse Blues
- Phoenix
- Picnic
- Piece o' Cake
- Pigs in Space
- Pinball
- Pitfall
- Pitfall II: Lost Caverns
- Planet Patrol
- Plaque Attack
- Poker Plus
- Polaris
- Pole Position
- Pong Sports
- Pooyan
- Popeye
- Porky's
- Pressure Cooker
- Private Eye
- Quadrun
- Q*Bert
- Q*Bert's Qubes
- Quest for Quintana Roo
- Quick Step
- Race
- Racquetball
- Radar
- Radar Lock
- Raft Rider
- Raiders of the Lost Ark
- Ram It
- Rampage
- Reactor
- Real Sports Baseball
- Real Sports Boxing
- Real Sports Football
- Real Sports Soccer
- Real Sports Tennis
- Real Sports Volleyball
- Rescue Terra I
- Revenge of the Beefsteak Tomatoes
- Riddle of the Sphinx
- River Patrol
- River Raid
- River Raid II
- Road Runner
- Robin Hood

- Robin Hood/Sir Lancelot
- Robot Tank
- Roc n Rope
- Room of Doom
- Rubik's Cube
- Scuba Diver
- Sea Hawk
- Sea Hunt
- Seamonster
- Seaquest
- Secret Quest
- Sentinel
- Shark Attack
- Shootin' Gallery
- Shuttle Orbiter
- Sir Lancelot
- Skate Boardin'
- Skeet Shoot
- Skiing
- Sky Diver
- Sky Skipper
- Slot Machine
- Slot Racers
- Slots
- Smurfs: Rescue in Gargamel's Castle
- Smurfs Save the Day
- Sneak n Peek
- Snoopy and the Red Baron
- Soccer
- Solar Fox
- Solar Storm
- Solaris
- Sorcerer
- Sorcerer's Apprentice
- Space Adventure
- Space Attack
- Space Canyon
- Space Cavern
- Spacechase
- Space Combat
- Space Invaders
- Space Jockey
- Spacemaster X-7
- Space Shuttle
- Space Tunnel
- Space War
- Speedway II
- Spelling
- Spiderdroid
- Spider Fighter
- Spider-Man
- Spider Maze
- Spike's Peak
- Spitfire Attack

- Springer
- Sprintmaster
- Spy Hunter
- Squeeze Box
- Sssnake
- Stampede
- Star Fox
- Stargate
- Stargunner
- Starmaster
- Star Raiders
- Star Ship
- Star Strike
- Star Trek: Strategic Operations Simulator
- Star Voyager
- Star Wars: Jedi Arena
- Star Wars: Return of the Jedi - Death Star Battle
- Star Wars: The Arcade Game
- Star Wars: The Empire Strikes Back
- Steeplechase
- Stellar Track
- Strategy X
- Strawberry Shortcake: Musical Matchups
- Street Racer
- Stronghold
- Stuntman
- Submarine Commander
- Sub Scan
- Subterranea
- Summer Games
- Super Baseball
- Super Breakout
- Super Challenge Baseball
- Super Challenge Football
- Super Cobra
- Super Football
- Superman
- Surround
- Survival Run
- Swordquest: Earthworld
- Swordquest: Fireworld
- Swordquest: Waterworld
- Tac-Scan
- Tank Brigade
- Tank Plus
- Tanks But No Tanks
- Tapeworm
- Tapper
- Target Fun
- Task Force
- Tax Avoiders

- Taz
- Tennis
- Texas Chainsaw Massacre
- Threshold
- Thunderground
- Time Pilot
- Time Warp
- Title Match Pro Wrestling
- Tomarc the Barbarian
- Tomcat: The F-14 Fighter Simulator
- Tooth Protectors
- Towering Inferno
- Track & Field
- Trick Shot
- Tron: Deadly Discs
- Tunnel Runner
- Turmoil
- Tutankham
- Universal Chaos
- Up n Down
- Vanguard
- Venture
- Video Checkers
- Video Chess
- Video Jogger
- Video Life
- Video Olympics
- Video Pinball
- Video Reflex
- Vulture Attack
- Wabbit
- Wall Ball
- Wall Defender
- Warlords
- Warplock
- Winter Games
- Wizard of Wor
- Word Zapper
- Worm War I
- Xenophobe
- X-Man
- Yars' Revenge
- Zaxxon
- Z-Tack

☐Bally Astrocade

RELEASE DATE	April 1978
DISCONTINUED	1983
ORIGINAL PRICE	$299
UNITS SOLD	N/A
BEST-SELLING GAME	N/A

The Bally Astrocade boasted a distinctive design with its silver and wood-grain finish. It featured a unique cartridge system that utilized "Game Packs," which were large cartridges that included multiple games on each cartridge. This novel concept offered players a variety of gaming experiences without the need for numerous individual cartridges.

The console came with a detachable controller, known as the "Bally Professional Arcade Controller" or "PAC." The PAC was a versatile input device that featured a numeric keypad, a joystick, and a red trigger button. This multifunctional controller allowed for complex gameplay and precise controls, making the Astrocade appealing to gaming enthusiasts seeking more advanced gaming experiences.

One of the standout features of the Bally Astrocade was its graphics and sound capabilities, which were impressive for its time. The console was capable of producing detailed graphics and vibrant colours, enhancing the visual appeal of its games. Additionally, it offered polyphonic sound, providing richer audio experiences compared to some of its competitors.

The Astrocade's game library consisted of a mix of original titles and licensed games. Notable titles included "Gunfight" (a Wild West shooter), "Muncher" (a Pac-Man-inspired game), and "Wizard of Wor" (a maze-based shooter). While the number of available games was relatively limited compared to other consoles, the quality and innovation of its games were well-regarded among players.

Despite its strengths, the Bally Astrocade faced challenges in the highly competitive video game market. Its marketing and distribution were not as widespread as some of its competitors, leading to limited visibility and a smaller user base. The console's relatively higher price point and the rise of other popular consoles further impacted its market penetration.

While the Bally Astrocade did not achieve the same commercial success as some of its contemporaries, the console remains appreciated by a devoted group of collectors and retro enthusiasts. Its innovative features, advanced capabilities, and "Game Packs" make it an intriguing artifact from the early days of gaming.

Games List

- 280 Zzzap / Dodgem
- Amazing Maze / Tic Tac Toe
- Artillery Duel
- Astro Battle
- Bally Pin
- Biorhythm
- Blackjack / Poker / Acey-Deucey
- Blast Droids
- Clowns / Brickyard
- Cosmic Raiders
- Dog Patch
- Elementary Math and Speed Math
- Football
- Galactic Invasion
- Galaxian
- Grand Prix / Demolition Derby
- Gun Fight
- The Incredible Wizard
- Letter Match / Spell'n Score / Crosswords
- Ms. CandyMan
- Muncher
- Panzer Attack / Red Baron
- Pirates Chase
- Sea Devil
- Seawolf / Missile
- Solar Conqueror
- Space Fortress
- Space Invaders
- Star Battle
- Tornado Baseball / Tennis / Hockey / Handball

☐APF-MP1000 Microcomputer System

RELEASE DATE	October 1978
DISCONTINUED	1981
ORIGINAL PRICE	$129.95
UNITS SOLD	>50,000
BEST-SELLING GAME	N/A

The APF-MP1000 Microcomputer System, released in 1978 by APF Electronics Inc., is an intriguing and versatile gaming console that holds a unique place in the early history of home computing and gaming. Combining the features of a gaming console and a personal computer, the APF-MP1000 offered users a diverse range of experiences and laid the groundwork for the convergence of gaming and computing.

The design of the APF-MP1000 was sleek and futuristic for its time, featuring a distinctive white and beige colour scheme with a detachable keyboard. It connected to the television through an RF switch, providing players with the option to access games and computing functions on their TV screens.

One of the key innovations of the APF-MP1000 was its built-in capabilities as a microcomputer. The console was equipped with a full keyboard and supported Basic programming language, allowing users to create and run their own programs, including games. This novel concept of combining gaming and programming capabilities made the APF-MP1000 stand out in the market.

The gaming library of the APF-MP1000 featured a variety of unique titles that showcased the system's capabilities. Games like "Space Destroyers" offered players engaging and enjoyable experiences. Additionally, the console supported cartridge-based gaming, expanding the gaming library further and providing access to additional exciting titles.

Beyond gaming, the APF-MP1000 served as an early home computer that provided educational and practical applications. Users could write and run their programs, learn coding skills, and perform basic computing tasks, making it a valuable educational tool.

The console's graphics and sound capabilities were modest but respectable for its time, offering players engaging visuals and audio. While not as advanced as some of its competitors, the APF-MP1000's gaming experiences and computing features were well-received by its user base.

Despite its innovative design and capabilities, the APF-MP1000 faced challenges in a highly competitive market dominated by other gaming consoles. The console's limited marketing and distribution impacted its visibility, leading to a smaller user base compared to some of its competitors.

Despite its relative obscurity, the APF-MP1000 remains a historically significant artifact in the early days of home computing and gaming. Its pioneering concept of merging gaming and computing in a single device foreshadowed the convergence of technologies in the future.

Games List

- MG1008 Backgammon
- MG1006 Baseball
- MG1007 Blackjack
- MG1004 Bowling/Micro Match
- MG1012 Boxing
- MG1005 Brickdown/Shooting Gallery
- MG1009 Casino I: Roulette/Keno/Slots
- MG1001/MG1002 Catena
- MG1003 Hangman/Tic Tac Toe/Doodle
- MG1011 Pinball/Dragon Hunt/Blockout
- MG1012 Space Destroyers
- MG1010 UFO/Sea Monster/Break It Down/Rebuild/Shoot

☐Interton VC4000

RELEASE DATE	1978
DISCONTINUED	1983
ORIGINAL PRICE	N/A
UNITS SOLD	N/A
BEST-SELLING GAME	N/A

The design of the Interton VC4000 was simple and straightforward, featuring a compact and lightweight console with a beige colour scheme. It connected to the television through an RF switch, allowing players to enjoy their gaming experiences on their TV screens.

The VC4000 utilized cartridges for its games, which expanded the gaming library and provided users with a variety of gaming experiences. However, the cartridges themselves were relatively basic, containing simple circuits that limited the complexity of the games compared to other consoles of its time.

The console's graphics and sound capabilities were modest, with monochrome visuals and basic audio effects. While not as advanced as some of its competitors, the VC4000's gaming experiences were enjoyable and entertaining for players seeking interactive entertainment in their homes.

One of the notable aspects of the Interton VC4000 was its educational potential. The console featured an expansion module called the "BASIC 4000," which allowed users to program and create their own games and applications using the BASIC programming language. This early foray into user-generated content was ahead of its time and offered users a glimpse into the future of interactive entertainment.

Despite its innovative features and early entry into the gaming market, the Interton VC4000 faced challenges in a competitive landscape dominated by more popular consoles. The North American video game crash of 1983 further impacted the industry, leading to a decline in the VC4000's sales and visibility.

Today, the Interton VC4000 remains a nostalgic artifact cherished by retro gaming enthusiasts and collectors interested in the early history of home video gaming. Its contributions to the evolving landscape of interactive entertainment, including its use of cartridges and user-generated content, continue to inspire the gaming industry's ongoing evolution.

Games List

- Air/Sea Battle
- Backgammon
- Basketball
- Blackjack
- Bowling/Ninepins
- Boxing Match
- Car Races
- Casino
- Chess
- Chess II
- Circus
- Cockpit
- Draughts
- Golf

- Hippodrome
- Hunting
- Hyperspace
- Intelligence I
- Intelligence II
- Intelligence III
- Intelligence IV/Reversi
- Invaders
- Mathematics I
- Mathematics II
- Melody/Simon
- Memory/Flag Capture
- Metropolis/Hangman
- Monster Man

- Motocross
- Outer Space Combat
- Paddle Games
- Pinball
- Rodeo (Unreleased)
- Soccer
- Solitaire
- Space Laser (Unreleased)
- Super Invaders
- Super-Space
- Tank Battle
- Winter Sports

☐Magnavox Odyssey 2

RELEASE DATE	EU: December 1978 (as the Philips Videopac G7000) USA: February 1979 JP: 1982 (as the Odyssey2) BR: 1983 (as the Philips Odyssey)
DISCONTINUED	1984
ORIGINAL PRICE	$179
UNITS SOLD	2 million
BEST-SELLING GAME	N/A

As the successor to the pioneering Magnavox Odyssey, the Odyssey 2 brought significant advancements and innovative features to the world of interactive entertainment.

The design of the Magnavox Odyssey 2 was sleek and compact, featuring a futuristic appearance with a silver and black color scheme. The console connected to the television through an RF switch, immersing players in a world of gaming on their TV screens.

One of the standout features of the Magnavox Odyssey 2 was its use of detachable keyboard overlays. These colourful, plastic overlays allowed players to interact with the games directly on the console's membrane keyboard, providing a unique and immersive gaming experience.

A defining aspect of the Magnavox Odyssey 2 was its innovative "Voice" module. This add-on peripheral provided speech synthesis, allowing games to include voice-based feedback and sound effects, enhancing the level of immersion and interactivity.

While the console's graphics and sound capabilities were modest by modern standards, they were impressive for its time. The Odyssey 2 offered colourful visuals and basic audio effects that complemented the gameplay and provided an enjoyable gaming experience.

Despite its innovative features and strong reception in the gaming community, the Magnavox Odyssey 2 faced challenges from more popular competitors in a competitive market. The video game industry's upheaval during the North American video game crash of 1983 also impacted the console's sales and market presence.

Games List

MAGNAVOX TITLES

- Alien Invaders - Plus!
- Alpine Skiing!
- Armored Encounter! / Subchase!
- Baseball!
- Blockout! / Breakdown!
- Bowling! / Basketball!
- Casino Slot Machine!
- Computer Intro!
- Computer Golf!
- Conquest of the World
- Cosmic Conflict!
- Dynasty!
- Electronic Table Soccer!
- Football!
- Freedom Fighters!
- Hockey! / Soccer!

- Invaders from Hyperspace!
- I've Got Your Number!
- K.C.'s Krazy Chase!
- K.C. Munchkin!
- Keyboard Creations!
- Killer Bees!
- Las Vegas Blackjack!
- Matchmaker! / Buzzword! / Logix!
- Monkeyshines!
- Nimble Numbers Ned!
- Out of this World! / Helicopter Rescue!
- P.T. Barnum's Acrobats!
- Pachinko!
- Pick Axe Pete!
- Pocket Billiards!

- Power Lords
- Quest for the Rings
- Gunfighter / Showdown in 2100 A.D.
- Sid the Spellbinder!
- Smithereens!
- Speedway! / Spin-out! / Cryptologic!
- Take the Money and Run!
- Attack of the Timelord!
- The Great Wall Street Fortune Hunt
- Thunderball!
- Turtles!
- Type & Tell!
- UFO!
- Volleyball!
- War of Nerves!

PHILIPS TITLES

- 4 in 1 Row
- A Labyrinth Game / Supermind
- Air Battle
- Air-Sea War / Battle
- American Football
- Backgammon
- Baseball
- Basket Game
- Battlefield
- Blackjack
- Blobbers
- Catch The Ball / Noughts and Crosses
- Chinese Logic
- Computer Programmer
- Conquest of the World (with accompanying board game)
- Cosmic Conflict
- Crazy Chase
- Dam Buster
- Depth Charge / Marksman
- Electronic Billiards
- Electronic Soccer / Electronic Ice Hockey
- Electronic Table Football
- Electronic Volleyball
- Flipper Game
- Freedom Fighters
- Golf
- Gunfighter
- Helicopter Rescue
- Jumping Acrobats
- Killer Bees
- Las Vegas Gambling
- Laser War
- Loony Balloon
- Mathematician / Echo

- Monkeyshines
- Morse
- Munchkin
- Musician (with musical keyboard)
- Neutron Star
- Nightmare
- Norseman
- Pairs / Space Rendezvous / Logic
- Pickaxe Pete
- Playschool Maths
- Race / Spin-Out / Cryptogram
- Samurai
- Satellite Attack
- Secret of the Pharaohs
- Skiing
- Space Monster
- Stone Sling
- Super Bee
- Take the Money and Run
- Tenpin Bowling / Basketball
- Terrahawks
- The Great Wall Street Fortune Hunt (with accompanying booklet and playing cards)
- The Mousing Cat

- The Quest of the Rings (with accompanying board game)
- Trans American Rally
- Turtles

BRAZIL RELEASE ONLY

- Clay Pigeon!
- Comando Noturno!

☐Mattel Intellivision

RELEASE DATE	USA: 1980
	UK: 1981
	ZA/DE/FRA/JP: 1982
	BR: 1983
DISCONTINUED	1990
ORIGINAL PRICE	$299
UNITS SOLD	>3 million
BEST-SELLING GAME	Las Vegas Poker & Blackjack

The Mattel Intellivision, released in 1980 by Mattel Electronics, is a trailblazing video game console that emerged as the main competitor to the Atari 2600. With its advanced technology, diverse gaming library, and unique peripherals, the Intellivision left a lasting impact on the gaming industry.

One of the defining features of the Intellivision was its innovative controller. The "Intellivision Master Component" came with detachable overlays that slid over the numeric keypad, transforming it into a versatile controller for each specific game. This innovation allowed for more complex gameplay and enhanced the gaming experience.

The Intellivision's game library showcased a mix of original titles and licensed games, with a focus on high-quality and sophisticated gameplay. Games like "Astrosmash," "BurgerTime," and "Tron: Deadly Discs" demonstrated the console's technical prowess and offered players engaging experiences that rivalled those of its competitors.

One of the standout aspects of the Mattel Intellivision was its innovative peripherals. The "Intellivoice" module provided speech synthesis, enabling voice-based gameplay feedback and sound effects in compatible games. Additionally, the "Intellivision Entertainment Computer System" (ECS) expanded the console's capabilities, transforming it into a home computer with a keyboard and data storage.

The Intellivision's graphics and sound capabilities were impressive for its time, surpassing those of the Atari 2600. Its visuals featured more detailed graphics and vibrant colours, elevating the gaming experience for players.

Games List

- ABPA Backgammon
- Advanced Dungeons & Dragons Cartridge
- Advanced Dungeons & Dragons: Treasure of Tarmin
- Armor Battle
- Astrosmash
- Atlantis
- Auto Racing
- B-17 Bomber (used Intellivoice)
- Beamrider
- Beauty & The Beast
- Big League Baseball
- Blockade Runner I
- Body Slam Super Pro Wrestling
- Bomb Squad (used Intellivoice)
- Bowling
- Boxing
- Bump 'N Jump
- BurgerTime
- Buzz Bombers
- Carnival
- Centipede
- Championship Tennis
- Checkers (released as "Draughts" in England)
- Chess
- Chip Shot: Super Pro Golf
- Circus
- Commando
- Slap Shot Super Pro Hockey
- Snafu
- Soccer
- Space Armada
- Space Battle
- Space Hawk
- Space Spartans (used Intellivoice)
- Spiker! Super Pro Volleyball
- Stadium Mud Buggies
- Stampede
- Star Strike
- Star Wars: The Empire Strikes Back
- Sub Hunt
- Super Cobra
- Super Pro Decathlon

- Congo Bongo
- Defender
- Demon Attack
- Dig Dug
- Diner
- Donkey Kong
- Donkey Kong Jr.
- Dracula
- Dragonfire
- Draughts
- Dreadnaught Factor, The
- The Electric Company Math Fun
- The Electric Company Word Fun
- Fathom
- Football
- Frog Bog
- Frogger
- Golf
- Happy Trails
- Hockey
- Horse Racing
- Hover Force
- Ice Trek
- Kool-Aid Man
- Lady Bug
- Las Vegas Poker & Blackjack (pack-in game)
- Las Vegas Roulette
- Learning Fun I
- Learning Fun II
- Lock 'N Chase
- Loco-Motion
- Major League Baseball
- Super Pro Football
- Swords & Serpents
- Tennis
- Thin Ice
- Thunder Castle
- Tower of Doom
- Triple Action
- Triple Challenge
- Tron Deadly Discs
- Tron Maze-a-Tron
- Tron: Solar Sailer (used Intellivoice)
- Tropical Trouble
- Truckin'
- Turbo
- Tutankham
- U.S. Ski Team Skiing
- USCF Chess
- Utopia

- Masters of the Universe: The Power of He-Man
- Micro League Baseball
- Microsurgeon
- Mind Strike
- Mission X
- Motocross
- Mountain Madness: Super Pro Skiing
- Mouse Trap
- NASL Soccer
- NBA Basketball
- NFL Football
- NHL Hockey
- Night Stalker
- Nova Blast
- Number Jumble
- Pac-Man
- PBA Bowling
- PGA Golf
- Pinball
- Pitfall!
- Pole Position
- Popeye
- Q*bert
- Reversi
- River Raid
- Royal Dealer
- Safecracker
- Sea Battle
- Sewer Sam
- Shark! Shark!
- Sharp Shot
- Slam Dunk Super Pro Basketball
- Vectron
- Venture
- White Water!
- World Championship Baseball
- Worm Whomper
- World Cup Football
- World Cup Soccer
- Zaxxon

INTELLIVISION KEYBOARD COMPONENT

- BASIC Programming Language (pack-in)
- Conversational French
- Crosswords I
- Crosswords II
- Crosswords III
- Family Budgeting
- Geography Challenge
- Jack LaLanne's Physical Conditioning
- Spelling Challenge

ENTERTAINMANENT COMPUTER SYSTEM

- Jetson's Way with Words
- Melody Blaster (music synthesizer add-on)
- Mr. Basic Meets Bits 'N Bytes
- Scooby Doo's Maze Chase
- World Series Major League Baseball (used Intellivoice)

☐ Intellivision Keyboard Component

☐ Intellivoice

☐ Entertainment Computer System

☐Epoch Cassette Vision

RELEASE DATE	JP: July 1981
DISCONTINUED	1984
ORIGINAL PRICE	$61 (¥13,500)
UNITS SOLD	400,000
BEST-SELLING GAME	N/A

The Epoch Cassette Vision, released in 1981 by the Japanese company Epoch, is a historically significant video game console that played a vital role in the early history of home gaming in Japan. As one of the first consoles developed in Japan, the Cassette Vision introduced a new era of interactive entertainment to Japanese households.

The design of the Epoch Cassette Vision was simple and utilitarian, featuring a compact and lightweight console with a white and light blue colour scheme. The Cassette Vision's most notable feature was its use of cassette tapes as game storage. Players inserted these cassette tapes into the console to access a selection of games.

One of the notable aspects of the Epoch Cassette Vision was its appeal to a younger audience. The console's games were often designed with simplicity and accessibility in mind, making it an ideal choice for family-friendly entertainment.

Despite its positive reception in Japan, the Cassette Vision faced challenges in the international gaming market. The global dominance of consoles like the Atari 2600 limited the Cassette Vision's visibility and market penetration outside of Japan.

Today, the Epoch Cassette Visions contributions to the early history of home video gaming in Japan and its role as a pioneer in the Japanese gaming industry are celebrated by gaming historians and enthusiasts.

As an influential console of its time, the Epoch Cassette Vision's legacy endures as a symbol of Japan's early gaming innovation and the creative strides that shaped the gaming experiences that captivate players worldwide.

Games List

- Astro Command
- Baseball
- Battle Vader
- Big Sports 12
- Elevator Panic
- Galaxian
- Grand Champion (unreleased)
- Kikori no Yosaku
- Monster Block
- Monster Mansion
- New Baseball
- PakPak

◻VTech CreatiVision

RELEASE DATE	1981
DISCONTINUED	1986
ORIGINAL PRICE	AU$295
UNITS SOLD	N/A
BEST-SELLING GAME	N/A

The VTech CreatiVision, released in 1981 by VTech Electronics, is a remarkable and versatile home computer and gaming console that made a significant impact during the early days of interactive entertainment. Combining the functionalities of a computer and a gaming system, the CreatiVision offered a diverse range of experiences to its users.

One of the standout features of the VTech CreatiVision was its dual functionality as both a gaming console and a home computer. The system came with a detachable keyboard that allowed users to perform computing tasks, write programs in BASIC, and access educational software.

The CreatiVision's game library showcased a mix of gaming experiences that catered to a wide audience. From arcade-style games to puzzle games, the console offered something for several types of players.

One of the defining aspects of the VTech CreatiVision was its focus on education. The system's educational software aimed to stimulate young minds and promote learning through interactive and engaging activities.

The CreatiVision's legacy endures as a symbol of VTech's commitment to innovation and creative strides in the gaming industry, and showcases Vtech's first steps into the gaming industry.

Games List

- ◻ Air/Sea Attack
- ◻ Astro Pinball
- ◻ Auto Chase
- ◻ Chopper Rescue
- ◻ Crazy Chicky
- ◻ Crazy Pucker
- ◻ Deep Sea Adventure
- ◻ Locomotive
- ◻ Mouse Puzzle
- ◻ Music Maker
- ◻ Planet Defender
- ◻ Police Jump
- ◻ Soccer
- ◻ Sonic Invader
- ◻ Stone Age
- ◻ Tank Attack
- ◻ Tennis

☐Emerson Arcadia 2001

RELEASE DATE	USA: May 1982
	JP: 1983
DISCONTINUED	1983
ORIGINAL PRICE	$99
UNITS SOLD	N/A
BEST-SELLING GAME	N/A

The Emerson Arcadia 2001, introduced in 1982 by Emerson Radio Corp., is a lesser-known but noteworthy video game console that made its mark in the early days of home gaming. As one of the early contenders in the second generation of gaming consoles, the Arcadia 2001 offered a range of gaming experiences and technical innovations.

One of the innovative features of the Emerson Arcadia 2001 was its unique and innovative controllers. The console came with detachable controllers that could be swapped for different game-specific keypads, enhancing the gameplay experience for each title. While ambitious, this concept did not gain widespread adoption among gaming enthusiasts.

The console's graphics and sound capabilities were on par with its competitors of the time, offering colourful visuals and basic audio effects that complemented the gameplay. While not as advanced as some of the leading consoles, the Arcadia 2001's technical capabilities were respectable and provided enjoyable gaming experiences.

Despite its technical innovations and varied gaming library, the Emerson Arcadia 2001 faced challenges in gaining traction in the competitive gaming market. The emergence of popular consoles like the Atari 2600 and the Mattel Intellivision limited the Arcadia 2001's visibility and market share.

Additionally, the video game industry experienced a downturn during the North American video game crash of 1983, further impacting the console's sales and potential for success.

While the Emerson Arcadia 2001 may not have achieved the same level of commercial success as some of its competitors, its legacy endures as a testament to the creative strides and innovations that shaped the early gaming landscape. As a symbol of the dynamic and competitive early gaming era, the Arcadia 2001 reminds us of the early pioneers who paved the way for the thriving and diverse gaming industry we enjoy today.

Games List

- 3D Attack
- 3-D Bowling
- 3-D Raceway
- 3-D Soccer
- Alien Invaders
- Astro Invader
- American Football
- Baseball
- Brain Quiz
- Breakaway
- Capture
- Cat Trax
- Circus
- Crazy Gobbler
- Crazy Climber
- Escape
- Funky Fish
- Galaxian
- Grand Prix 3-D
- Grand Slam Tennis
- Hobo
- Home Squadron
- Horse Racing
- Jump Bug
- Jungler
- Kidou Senshi Gundamu (Japan)
- Math Logic
- Missile War
- Ocean Battle
- Pleiades
- RD2 Tank
- Red Clash
- Robot Killer
- Route 16
- Soccer
- Space Attack
- Space Chess
- Space Mission
- Space Raiders
- Space Squadron
- Space Vultures
- Spiders
- Star Chess
- Super Bug
- Super Gobbler
- Tanks A Lot
- The End
- Turtles/Turpin

☐ColecoVision

RELEASE DATE	USA: August 1982
	EU: July 1983
DISCONTINUED	1985
ORIGINAL PRICE	$175
UNITS SOLD	>2 million
BEST-SELLING GAME	Donkey Kong

The Colecovision came to be as a result of the ambition and vision of Coleco Industries, a company initially known for producing leather supplies. In the late 1970s, the video game industry was experiencing significant growth with the success of consoles like the Atari 2600. Seeing the potential in the burgeoning video game market, Coleco decided to enter the gaming industry.

In 1982, Coleco released the Colecovision, positioning it as a direct competitor to the Atari 2600. The company aimed to distinguish the Colecovision by offering superior graphics and arcade-quality gaming experiences. To achieve this, Coleco secured licensing deals with popular arcade game developers, most notably acquiring the rights to "Donkey Kong," a highly acclaimed arcade game developed by Nintendo.

By securing the rights to "Donkey Kong," Coleco could bundle the game with the Colecovision. This strategic move significantly boosted the console's appeal to gamers, as "Donkey Kong" was a massive hit in arcades, and players now had the opportunity to experience it at home.

Coleco invested in developing a powerful console with advanced hardware capabilities. The Colecovision's hardware allowed it to render detailed graphics and produce more sophisticated sound effects compared to its competitors. This technical superiority was showcased in its arcade game conversions, enhancing the overall gaming experience and further differentiating the Colecovision from other consoles in the market.

In addition to its technical prowess, the Colecovision came with a unique controller that featured a numeric keypad, a joystick, and action buttons. This versatile controller allowed for precise control in various gaming genres, making it well-suited for both arcade and console-style games.

Upon its release, the Colecovision received critical acclaim and was well-received by gamers. It became a commercial success and quickly gained a strong following. The console's library of games continued to expand, further solidifying its position in the gaming industry.

Despite its success, the Colecovision faced challenges in the form of the video game market crash in 1983. The crash had a significant impact on the gaming industry, leading to a decline in sales for many console manufacturers, including Coleco.

Games List

- 2010: The Graphic Action Game
- Alcazar: The Forgotten Fortress
- Alphabet Zoo
- Amazing Bumpman
- Antarctic Adventure
- Aquattack
- Artillery Duel
- Artillery Duel/Chuck Norris Superkicks ("Double-Ender")
- B.C.'s Quest for Tires
- B.C. II: Grog's Revenge
- Beamrider
- Blockade Runner
- Boulder Dash
- Brain Strainers
- Buck Rogers: Planet of Zoom
- Bump 'n' Jump
- BurgerTime
- Cabbage Patch Kids: Adventures in the Park
- Cabbage Patch Kids Picture Show
- Campaign '84
- Carnival
- Centipede
- Choplifter!
- Chuck Norris Superkicks
- Congo Bongo
- Cosmic Avenger
- Cosmic Crisis
- The Dam Busters
- Dance Fantasy
- Decathlon
- Defender
- Destructor
- Dig Dug
- Donkey Kong
- Donkey Kong Jr.
- Dr. Seuss' Fix-Up the Mix-Up Puzzler
- Dragonfire
- The Dukes of Hazzard
- Evolution
- Facemaker
- Fathom
- Flipper Slipper
- Fortune Builder
- Fraction Fever
- Frenzy
- Frogger
- Frogger II: Threeedeep!
- Galaxian
- Gateway to Apshai
- Gorf
- Gust Buster
- Gyruss
- H.E.R.O.
- The Heist
- Illusions
- It's Only Rock 'N Roll
- James Bond 007
- Jukebox
- Jumpman Jr.
- Jungle Hunt
- Ken Uston Blackjack/Poker
- Keystone Kapers
- Kung Fu Superkicks
- Lady Bug
- Learning with Leeper
- Linking Logic
- Logic Levels
- Looping
- Lord of the Dungeon
- Memory Manor
- Meteoric Shower
- Miner 2049er
- Monkey Academy
- Montezuma's Revenge
- Moonsweeper
- Motocross Racer
- Motocross Racer/Tomarc the Barbarian ("Double-Ender")
- Mountain King
- Mouse Trap
- Mr. Do!
- Mr. Do!'s Castle
- Ms. Space
- Nova Blast
- Oil's Well
- Omega Race
- One on One Basketball
- Pac-Man
- Pepper II
- Pitfall!
- Pitfall II: Lost Caverns
- Pitstop
- Popeye
- Power Lords
- Q*bert
- Q*bert's Qubes
- Quest for Quintana Roo
- River Raid
- Robin Hood
- Robin Hood/Sir Lancelot ("Double-Ender")
- Roc 'N Rope Rock 'N Bolt
- Rocky Super Action Boxing
- Rolloverture
- Root Beer Tapper
- Sammy Lightfoot
- Sector Alpha
- Sewer Sam
- Sir Lancelot
- Skiing
- Slither
- Slurpy
- Smurf Paint 'n' Play Workshop
- Smurf: Rescue in Gargamel's Castle
- Space Fury
- Space Panic
- Spectron
- Spy Hunter
- Squish 'Em Featuring Sam
- Star Trek: Strategic Operations Simulator
- Star Wars: The Arcade Game
- Steamroller
- Strike It
- SubRoc
- Super Action Baseball
- Super Action Football
- Super Action Soccer
- Super Cobra
- Super Crossforce
- Tank Wars
- Tarzan
- Telly Turtle
- Threshold
- Time Pilot
- Tomarc the Barbarian
- Tournament Tennis
- Turbo
- Tutankham
- Up'n Down
- Venture
- Victory
- WarGames
- War Room
- Wing War
- The Wizard of Id's Wiz Math
- Word Feud
- Zaxxon
- Zenji

☐ ColecoVision Expansion Module #1

☐ ColecoVision Expansion Module #2

☐ ColecoVision Expansion Module #3

☐SHG Black Point

RELEASE DATE	DE: 1982
DISCONTINUED	N/A
ORIGINAL PRICE	168DM
UNITS SOLD	N/A
BEST-SELLING GAME	N/A

The SHG Black Point is a second-generation home video game console that made its debut in 1982. It was exclusively released in Germany by Süddeutsche Elektro-Hausgeräte (SHG).

This gaming system came with two detachable game controllers, each equipped with an analog joystick and a fire button. Additionally, the console featured 10 buttons used for selecting games stored on ROM cartridges. On the console's housing, there was also a difficulty switch, an on/off switch, and a start button. The two models of the console are named FS-1003 and FS-2000, both falling under the SHG Black Point series.

The gaming library for the SHG Black Point includes very few officially known titles, all stored on ROM cartridges. The games were sold separately, with prices ranging from 50 to 80 DEM. Interestingly, although the console itself lacks a CPU or any RAM, the cartridges themselves contain the necessary computing components. A notable inclusion with the console is a module that offers 10 different variations of the classic game Pong.

Games List

- 1000-Treffer-Spiel (1000 Hit Game)
- Grand Prix
- Motorradrennen (Motorcycle Race)
- Panzerschlacht (Tank Battle)
- Schützenspiel (Shooter Game)
- Seekrieg (Naval War)
- Zehn elektronische Fernsehspiele in Farbe (Ten Color Electronic TV Games)

☐Atari 5200

RELEASE DATE	USA: November 1982
DISCONTINUED	May 1984
ORIGINAL PRICE	$270
UNITS SOLD	>1 million
BEST-SELLING GAME	N/A

The Atari 5200 is a video game console released by Atari, Inc. in 1982 as a successor to the popular Atari 2600. It was designed to be a more advanced and powerful gaming system, offering improved graphics and gameplay compared to its predecessor. However, despite its promising features, the Atari 5200 faced both critical and commercial challenges during its lifespan.

The Atari 5200 had a sleek and futuristic design, featuring a large console with a silver and black colour scheme. It came with detachable controllers that had a distinctive trapezoidal shape and a numeric keypad, offering players more control options. Additionally, the controllers featured a joystick and multiple action buttons to enhance gameplay possibilities.

One of the notable features of the Atari 5200 was its capability to provide better graphics and sound compared to the Atari 2600. The system had more powerful hardware and graphics capabilities, enabling developers to create more visually impressive games.

Despite its promising features, the Atari 5200 faced some technical issues that affected its reputation. The console had a non-centring joystick, which often led to control problems during gameplay. Additionally, the early versions of the console had reliability issues, leading to the creation of a revised model with improvements.

The timing of the Atari 5200's release was unfortunate. The video game market experienced a downturn in the early 1980s due to factors like an oversaturated market, competition from other gaming consoles, and a lack of quality control in the gaming industry. These challenges impacted the Atari 5200's commercial success.

Games List

- The Activision Decathlon
- Astro Chase
- Ballblazer
- Beamrider
- Berzerk
- Blue Print
- Bounty Bob Strikes Back
- Buck Rogers: Planet of Zoom
- Centipede
- Choplifter!
- Congo Bongo
- Countermeasure
- Defender
- Dig Dug
- The Dreadnaught Factor
- Frogger
- Frogger II: Threeedeep!
- Galaxian
- Gorf
- Gremlins
- Gyruss
- H.E.R.O.
- James Bond 007
- Joust
- Jungle Hunt
- K-Razy Shootout
- Kaboom!
- Kangaroo Kapers
- Mario Bros.
- Megamania
- Meteorites
- Miner 2049er
- Missile Command
- Montezuma's Revenge
- Moon Patrol
- Mountain King
- Mr. Do!'s Castle
- Ms. Pac-Man
- Pac-Man
- Pengo
- Pitfall!
- Pitfall II: Lost Caverns
- Pole Position
- Popeye
- Q*Bert
- Qix
- Quest for Quintana Roo
- Real Sports Baseball
- Real Sports Football
- Real Sports Soccer
- Real Sports Tennis Rescue on Fractalus!
- River Raid
- Robotron: 2084
- Space Dungeon
- Space Invaders
- Space Shuttle
- Star Raiders
- Star Trek: Strategic Operations Simulator
- Star Wars: Return of the Jedi - Death Star Battle
- Star Wars: The Arcade Game
- Super Breakout
- Super Cobra
- Vanguard
- Wizard of Wor
- Zaxxon
- Zenji
- Zone Ranger

Vectrex

RELEASE DATE	USA: November 1982
	EU: May 1983
	JP: June 1983
DISCONTINUED	February 1984
ORIGINAL PRICE	$199
UNITS SOLD	N/A
BEST-SELLING GAME	N/A

The Vectrex was a unique and innovative video game console released in 1982 by General Consumer Electronics (GCE), and later sold by Milton Bradley. It stood out from other gaming systems of its time due to its vector-based graphics, built-in screen, and self-contained design, making it one of the first and only home video game consoles with a built-in display.

The Vectrex had a built-in 9-inch monochrome vector display, which was an unusual feature at the time, as most other consoles required connection to a separate television set for gameplay.

The console came with a single wired controller, which featured a joystick and a set of buttons for gameplay. The vector display technology allowed for sharp and precise graphics, giving games a unique visual style compared to the pixel-based graphics of other gaming consoles.

The Vectrex had a small but impressive library of games. Since the console's graphics were vector-based, developers could create games with lines and shapes that were much more detailed and fluid compared to traditional raster-based graphics. Some of the most notable games for the Vectrex included "Armor Attack," "Mine Storm," "Space Wars," "Spike," and "Star Castle."

Additionally, the Vectrex had a unique feature called the "Light Pen," which allowed players to interact directly with the screen by pointing at specific locations. This was used in a few games and provided an innovative and interactive gameplay experience.

While the Vectrex was praised for its unique design and vector graphics, it faced challenges in the market. The console was released during the video game crash, and its high price and limited game library contributed to its commercial struggles.

As a result, the Vectrex had a relatively short lifespan, and production ceased in 1984. However, despite its brief time on the market, the console left a lasting impact on gaming enthusiasts and collectors. The Vectrex is highly regarded today for its unique gaming experience, its innovative vector display technology, and its contributions to the evolution of video game graphics.

The Vectrex's legacy endures as a niche and sought-after collectible, with retro gaming enthusiasts cherishing the console for its historical significance and its representation of a fascinating era in the gaming industry.

Games List

3D Crazy Coaster	Fortress of Narzod	Scramble
3D Mine Storm	Heads Up	Solar Quest
3D Narrow Escape	Hyperchase	Space Wars
AnimAction	Melody Master	Spike
Armor Attack	Mine Storm	Spinball
Art Master	Mine Storm 2	Star Castle
Bedlam	Mine Storm III	Star Hawk
Berzerk	Mr. Boston	Star Trek: The Motion
Blitz!	Polar Rescue	Picture
Clean Sweep	Pole Position	Web Wars
Cosmic Chasm	Rip Off	

☐Gakken Compact Vision TV Boy

RELEASE DATE	JP: October 1983
DISCONTINUED	N/A
ORIGINAL PRICE	¥8,800
UNITS SOLD	N/A
BEST-SELLING GAME	N/A

The Gakken Compact Vision TV Boy emerged as a second-generation home video game console developed by Gakken. It made its debut in Japan in 1983, hitting the market with a price tag of ¥8,800.

The console's primary aim was to challenge the Epoch Cassette Vision, which had a strong grip on 70% of the Japanese gaming market at that time.

Unfortunately, the Gakken Compact Vision TV Boy faced significant competition from the Nintendo Famicom and Sega SG-1000, both of which offered more advanced features and larger game libraries despite their higher price points (¥15,000). Additionally, Epoch had recently launched the Cassette Vision Jr. revision, priced at just ¥5,000. These factors rendered the Gakken console relatively obsolete from the outset.

The system struggled to gain momentum due to its high price, limited and relatively basic game selection, and an unconventional form factor. As a result, it experienced lackluster sales performance. These circumstances have since elevated its status as a highly sought-after and rare collector's item among retro gaming enthusiasts.

Games List

- [ ] Excite Invader
- [ ] Mr. Bomb
- [ ] Robotan Wars
- [ ] *Chitaikū Daisakusen* (Big operation of surface-to-air')
- [ ] Frogger
- [ ] Shigaisen 200X-nen (warfare year 200X')

Handheld Consoles

Milton Bradley Microvision

RELEASE DATE	November 1979
DISCONTINUED	1981
ORIGINAL PRICE	$49.99
UNITS SOLD	N/A
BEST-SELLING GAME	N/A

In the late 1970s, the electronic gaming industry was primarily dominated by arcade games and home consoles like the Atari 2600. Jay Smith, an engineer and inventor, had a vision of creating a handheld gaming device that could offer a variety of games without being tied to a single built-in game.

Smith teamed up with Milton Bradley Company, a well-established board game and toy manufacturer, to bring his idea to life. The collaboration resulted in the birth of the Microvision.

The Milton Bradley Microvision is widely recognized as the first handheld game console with interchangeable cartridges, setting the stage for future handheld gaming devices.

The Microvision featured a small LCD screen (approximately 16x16 pixels) and a collection of interchangeable game cartridges. The console itself had a simple directional pad and action buttons to control the games. The console's initial release came with a small but diverse selection of game cartridges, showcasing the system's potential.

The Microvision was an ambitious concept for its time, allowing players to change games by inserting different cartridges into the console. This was a groundbreaking innovation that laid the groundwork for the handheld gaming market that would flourish in the following decades.

Despite its innovative design, the Microvision faced challenges. The technology of the time limited the display resolution and graphics quality. Additionally, the cost of the cartridges and the console itself made it a relatively expensive gaming option.

These factors, combined with competition from other gaming systems, contributed to its limited commercial success.

Eventually, the Microvision was discontinued after a relatively short run, but its impact on the gaming industry was significant. It inspired the development of more advanced handheld gaming devices, including the iconic Nintendo Game Boy, which was released in 1989 and went on to become one of the most successful and influential handheld gaming consoles of all time.

Games List

- Alien Raiders
- Barrage (unreleased)
- Baseball
- Blockbuster
- Bowling
- Connect Four
- Cosmic Hunter
- Mindbuster Pinball
- Sea Duel
- Star Trek: Phaser Strikes
- Super Blockbuster
- Vegas Slots

☐Nintendo Game & Watch

RELEASE DATE	April 1980
DISCONTINUED	1991
ORIGINAL PRICE	N/A
UNITS SOLD	43.4 million
BEST-SELLING GAME	Donkey Kong

The Nintendo Game & Watch is a line of handheld electronic games and timekeeping devices produced by Nintendo. It was one of Nintendo's early successes and laid the groundwork for their future ventures in the handheld gaming market.

The story behind the Nintendo Game & Watch begins with the success of Nintendo in the arcade game industry during the late 1970s. Nintendo, founded in 1889 as a playing card company, had evolved into a toy and game manufacturer by the mid-20th century.

In 1979, Gunpei Yokoi, an engineer working for Nintendo, came up with the idea for a portable handheld game that would fit into the palm of a hand. The concept was inspired by observing a businessman playing with an LCD calculator during a train ride. Yokoi believed that by integrating a game into a similarly portable device, Nintendo could create a new and exciting form of entertainment.

Nintendo's president, Hiroshi Yamauchi, liked Yokoi's idea and gave him the green light to develop the concept further. The first game Yokoi created for the handheld device was called "Ball," a juggling game that served as a proof of concept. The game was simple yet addictive, and Yamauchi saw its potential.

The final design of the handheld device featured a small LCD screen and a directional pad (D-pad) for controls. This design allowed players to interact with the game and provided a more immersive experience than typical LCD games of that time.

In 1980, Nintendo officially launched the product as the "Game & Watch" series. The name "Game & Watch" referred to the device's dual functionality—it was a handheld game and also featured a digital watch with an alarm function. Each Game & Watch device came with a built-in game, and the LCD screen displayed characters and simple graphics.

The series started with the release of the "Ball" game, which involved juggling balls, and it was an instant hit. Over the next decade, Nintendo produced and released a wide range of Game & Watch titles, with games spanning various genres such as action, sports, puzzle, and more.

One of the most famous Game & Watch titles was "Donkey Kong," released in 1982. It was the first game in the series to feature dual screens, with one screen displaying the main gameplay and the other showing the player's score.

The Game & Watch series eventually sold over 43 million units worldwide, making it a significant success for Nintendo and laying the foundation for their future ventures in the handheld gaming market.

The success of the Game & Watch series solidified Nintendo's position as a leading player in the gaming industry. popularity of these devices helped pave the way for Nintendo's future handheld consoles, such as the iconic Game Boy, which was released in 1989 and became a massive commercial success. As technology advanced and handheld gaming devices evolved, Nintendo eventually discontinued the Game & Watch line in the early 1990s.

Games List

Silver
- Ball
- Fire
- Flagman
- Judge
- Vermin

Gold
- Helmet
- Lion
- Manhole

Wide Screen
- Chef
- Egg
- Fire Attack
- Mickey Mouse
- Octopus
- Parachute
- Popeye
- Snoopy Tennis
- Soccer (Unreleased)
- Turtle Bridge

Multi-Screen
- Black Jack
- Bombsweeper
- Donkey Kong
- Donkey Kong II
- Gold Cliff
- Green House
- Life Boat
- Mario Bros.
- Mickey & Donald
- Oil Panic
- Pinball
- Rain Shower
- Safebuster
- Squish
- Zelda

New Wide Screen
- Balloon Fight
- Climber
- Donkey Kong Jr.
- Mario the Juggler
- Mario's Cement Factory
- Super Mario Bros.
- Tropical Fish

Tabletop
- Donkey Kong Jr.
- Mario's Cement Factory
- Popeye

SnoopyPanorama
- Snoopy
- Popeye
- Donkey Kong Jr.
- Mario's Bombs Away
- Mickey Mouse
- Donkey Kong Circus

Super Color
- Spitball Sparky
- Crab Grab

Micro Vs.
- Boxing
- Donkey Kong 3
- Donkey Kong Hockey

Crystal Screen
- Super Mario Bros.
- Climber
- Balloon Fight

☐Entex Select-A-Game

RELEASE DATE	1981
DISCONTINUED	1982
ORIGINAL PRICE	$59
UNITS SOLD	N/A
BEST-SELLING GAME	N/A

The Entex Select-A-Game is a handheld electronic gaming device produced by the American toy company Entex Industries Inc. during the early 1980s. It was one of the early attempts at creating a handheld gaming console that offered multiple games in a single device.

The Select-A-Game featured a compact design resembling a small pocket calculator, and it came with a built-in LCD screen and various control buttons. The device allowed players to switch between different games by inserting a game cartridge into a slot located on the back of the device.

Entex released several different game cartridges for the Select-A-Game, each containing unique games. The games included various genres, such as sports, arcade-style, and puzzle games. While the graphics and gameplay were relatively simple compared to modern standards, they were impressive for the time and provided enjoyable entertainment for users.

The Entex Select-A-Game found moderate success in the handheld gaming market, competing with other early handheld devices like the Nintendo Game & Watch and Milton Bradley Microvision. However, as technology continued to advance, more advanced and feature-rich handheld gaming consoles, such as the Nintendo Game Boy, entered the market and eventually overshadowed the Select-A-Game.

As a result, the Entex Select-A-Game was eventually discontinued, and it is now considered a collector's item among retro gaming enthusiasts.

Games List

- ☐ Baseball 4
- ☐ Basketball 3
- ☐ Battleship (unreleased)

- ☐ Football 4
- ☐ Pacman 2
- ☐ Pinball

- ☐ Space Invader 2
- ☐ Turtles (unreleased)

☐Entex Adventure Vision

RELEASE DATE	1982
DISCONTINUED	1983
ORIGINAL PRICE	$79.95
UNITS SOLD	10,000 - 50,757
BEST-SELLING GAME	N/A

The Adventure Vision featured a reflective, monochromatic display system known as "catadioptric" optics. This innovative technology allowed the device to produce colour-like graphics without using traditional colour screens or colour overlays. Instead, it relied on a combination of mirrors, lenses, and light to create the illusion of colours, resulting in a more immersive gaming experience for players.

One of the main selling points of the Adventure Vision was the four built-in games that came pre-installed on the device.

The Adventure Vision's unique technology garnered attention upon its release. However, it faced stiff competition from other gaming devices. The Adventure Vision's higher price, limited game library, and its unconventional design led to modest sales, ultimately leading to its discontinuation within a year of its release. As a result, the Adventure Vision became a rare and sought-after collectible among retro gaming enthusiasts.

Games List

- Defender
- Space Force
- Super Cobra
- Turtles

☐Palmtex Portable Videogame System/Super Micro

RELEASE DATE	May 1984
DISCONTINUED	1985
ORIGINAL PRICE	$39.95
UNITS SOLD	<37,200
BEST-SELLING GAME	N/A

The Palmtex Super Micro was a handheld gaming device released by Palmtex, a company known for producing electronic gaming consoles and other electronic products in the 1980s.

Only three games are known to have been released on the Super Micro. Due to an issue with poor screen brightness, Palmtex released a 'LightPak' to illuminate the screen better. The console was a victim of the 1983 video game crash, resulting in a product being released into an already-saturated market.

Games List

- Aladdin's Adventures
- Outflank
- React Attack

☐Epoch Game Pocket Computer

RELEASE DATE	JP: November 1984
DISCONTINUED	N/A
ORIGINAL PRICE	¥12,800
UNITS SOLD	N/A
BEST-SELLING GAME	N/A

The Epoch Game Pocket Computer (often referred to simply as the Game Pocket Computer or GPC) is a handheld gaming device produced by the Japanese company Epoch Co., Ltd.

Although the Epoch Game Pocket Computer was technologically impressive for its time, it faced stiff competition from other handheld gaming devices, such as the Nintendo Game & Watch and the Milton Bradley Microvision. ts price and the limitations of its monochromatic display hindered its commercial success outside of Japan.

As a result, the Epoch Game Pocket Computer remained more popular in its home country of Japan, although eventually the console gained a dedicated following among collectors and retro gaming enthusiasts worldwide.

Games List

- ☐ Puzzle Game (パズルゲーム, Pazurugēmu) (Built-in)
- ☐ Graphics function (グラフィック機能, Gurafikku kinō) (built-in)
- ☐ Astro Bomber (アストロボンバー, Asutorobombā)
- ☐ Block Maze (ブロックメイズ, Burokkumeizu)
- ☐ Pocket Computer Mahjong (ポケコンマージャン, Pokekonmājyan)
- ☐ Pocket Computer Reversi (ポケコンリバーシ, Pokekonribāsi)
- ☐ Sokoban (倉庫番, sōko-ban)

☐Bandai Digi Casse

RELEASE DATE	JP: 1984
	EU: 1986
DISCONTINUED	N/A
ORIGINAL PRICE	N/A
UNITS SOLD	N/A
BEST-SELLING GAME	N/A

During the 1980s, several toy and gaming companies, including Bandai, released various handheld electronic games to cater to the growing demand for portable entertainment. These handheld devices often focused on providing basic games inspired by arcade classics or popular themes of the time.

The Digi Casse was originally released in 1984, and featured a small selection of games. Each of the Digi Casse's eight games had their own built-in LCD screen in an attempt to capitalize on the Nintendo Game & Watch's popularity.

Games List

JP Releases

- ☐ City Turbo Race シティターボレース, Shititāborēsu)
- ☐ Express home delivery 宅急便, Takkyūbin)
- ☐ Hageransu ハゲランス, Hageransu)
- ☐ Mt. Fuji explosion 富士山大爆発, Fujiyama daibakuhatsu)

EU Releases

- ☐ Pelican
- ☐ Penguin
- ☐ Submarine
- ☐ Frogs & Insects

About The Author

I have been a keen gaming enthusiast for most of my life. I can still remember the first video game I ever played: Colin McRae Rally 2.0 on the PC. Not only did this introduce me to another passion (cars), it also opened my eyes to the wide world of video gaming. My first console was a Game Boy Color, and (like a lot of people my age), I spent half my time playing Pokémon. My brother and I eventually received a Nintendo GameCube one Christmas – this exact console is still a part of my personal collection, and is one of the few gaming items I would refuse to ever part with.

I became a collector in my teenage years. I would spend hours going to local independent stores looking for that specific game, console or accessory. I eventually took a job in one of these stores, and spent three years learning more about retro gaming, as well as retro toys and other collectibles. Like many others, my gaming collection is a hobby and a passion that continues to excite me to this day.

I decided to write this book so that others may also learn about the rich history surrounding video gaming, and about the forgotten consoles that could've been but never were.